THE P

THE PARIS HUSBAND

How It Really Was Between Ernest and Hadley Hemingway

SCOTT DONALDSON

Simply Charly

New York

This book is for Janet Breckenridge and Britton Donaldson

CONTENTS

PRAISE FOR *THE PARIS HUSBAND*

"Ever since Ernest Hemingway's *A Moveable Feast* was published in 1964 two generations of readers have been fascinated by the eternal romance of Ernest and Hadley, a never-ending love story. The narrative has been recounted and analyzed in biography and fiction leaving a responsive audience yearning for more. Here comes *The Paris Husband*, a spellbinding account of the writer's first marriage, its breakup and the lifelong impact it would have upon Hemingway and his writing. A seasoned author and Hemingway scholar, Scott Donaldson brings this remarkable story to life with precision, lending keen new insight into Hemingway's elusive character. A masterful work and a cracking good read."

—Valerie Hemingway, author of *Running With the Bulls: My Years with the Hemingways*

"If there were a Mount Rushmore of Hemingway

scholars, Scott Donaldson would belong. This lucid, engaging history of Hemingway's first marriage only enhances that legendary reputation. Donaldson is a perfect guide through this often mysterious period in the young Hemingway's career. It is essential reading for anyone interested in Hemingway's first steps on the international stage."

—Mark Cirino, co-editor of *Hemingway and Italy: 21st Century Perspectives* and editor of the Reading Hemingway Series

"Accuracy can be fascinating. Scott Donaldson's clear and simply focused narrative rings true. I like his reversal of the earlier title (Paula McLain's *The Paris Wife*) because he makes all too clear that Ernest Hemingway was the central persona in the marriage with Hadley Richardson. Riveting."

—Linda Wagner-Martin, author of *Hemingway's Wars: Public and Private Battles*

"The story of Ernest Hemingway's first marriage to Hadley Richardson has been recounted in countless biographies and spun into fable in popular fiction. It's a powerful story because Hemingway's love for Hadley was an essential gauge of his artistic trajectory. From romanticized scenes of young expatriate love to stolen manuscripts in a Parisian train station to the appearance on the slopes of Schruns of a third who would upset the couple's equanimity Hemingway returned compulsively to moments in the relationship to try to understand when and why he betrayed the values for which his writing and his life stood. Scott Donaldson's *The Paris Husband* is a wonderful book that does us the immense favor of separating certifiable facts from the inevitable conjecture and dramatizing that have come to encrust these scenes from a marriage. With clear-eyed tenacity and a gracious empathy toward both sides, Donaldson shows that at their core Ernest and Hadley shared an intimate friendship and genuine affection that not even a divorce could end. This is a beautiful piece of storytelling by one of our best American biographers."

—Kirk Curnutt, author of *Coffee with Hemingway* and *A Reader's Guide to Hemingway's To Have and Have Not*

"Separating fact from fiction, Scott Donaldson has deftly reconstructed the story that filled the older Ernest Hemingway with remorse—the narrative of his magical, doomed marriage to Hadley during the early years in Paris. Donaldson offers an inside view of Hemingway's work as a journalist and handles two vexed episodes, Hadley's loss of the early manuscripts and Pauline's infiltration into their lives, with admirable balance. As a renowned scholar-biographer, he makes brilliant use of the author's notebooks and drafts to deliver fresh insights into Hemingway's assessments of blame—final judgments that neither version of *A Moveable Feast* can fully convey. Anyone who wants to understand how that first marriage broke apart and changed a troubled literary life will find this an irresistible read."

—J. Gerald Kennedy, author of *Imagining Paris*

"Drawing expertly on his many years reading, researching, and teaching that have produced five books entirely or partially about Hemingway, Scott Donaldson gives us here the most authoritative account of the complex courtship, marriage, and divorce of Hadley Richardson and Ernest Hemingway. Deftly and effectively utilizing all the relevant secondary and primary source materials—some of the latter previously unpublished—Donaldson debunks myths promulgated by previous biographers and critics, setting the record straight in a fascinating and highly readable narrative that will be as revelatory for Hemingway fans as for those previously unfamiliar with the story of his first marriage."

—Jackson R. Bryer, President and co-founder of F. Scott Fitzgerald Society and co-editor of *French Connections: Hemingway and Fitzgerald Abroad*

"In *The Paris Husband*, preeminent literary biographer and respected Hemingway scholar, Scott Donaldson sets the record straight about Ernest Hemingway's precious, tumultuous—and legendary—Paris years. Drawing upon his detailed knowledge of Hemingway's biography as well as his deep understanding of Hemingway's personality, Donaldson offers readers a compelling and compassionate glimpse of Hemingway as husband that helps humanize the iconic author and this mythic period of his development."

—Suzanne del Gizzo, Editor of *The Hemingway Review*

INTRODUCTION

On the evening of December 3, 1922, Hadley Hemingway went to the Gare de Lyon in Paris to take the overnight train to Lausanne, Switzerland, where her husband Ernest was covering the international peace conference negotiating the end of the Greco-Turkish War. Ernest had been urging Hadley to come, and she would have made the trip sooner but for a lingering bout with the flu. Now she was on her way, and happy at the prospect of reuniting with the young man (23 years old to her 31) she had married two years earlier and was very much in love with.

In preparing for the trip, Hadley packed a suitcase with clothes to last through the winter skiing months she and Ernest were planning to spend in Chamby-sur-Montreux, a resort overlooking Lake Geneva, about 20 miles from Lausanne. As a surprise for Ernest, she also gathered up the unpublished stories, poems, and draft of a novel he'd been working on, putting these papers in a separate

1

valise. He could show some of that writing to Lincoln Steffens, the famous former muckraker also covering the Lausanne Conference, who had taken an interest in Hemingway's future. And Ernest could do some revising during their stay in the mountains. This, it turned out, was a terrible mistake.

At the train station, a porter helped Hadley find an unoccupied compartment. He placed her suitcase on the top of the luggage rack and the valise on a lower shelf. She was early, as she hadn't wanted to risk getting caught in traffic and missing her train, so she left the bags where they were and went out to buy a sandwich and some Evian water. When she got back, the suitcase was still in its place, but the valise was gone—stolen, presumably, by a thief soon to be disillusioned by its contents. Desperately, Hadley told the conductor what had happened, but there was really nothing else to do. The valise, and the serious writing Ernest had done during their year in Europe, was gone. She rode the long journey to Lausanne in sleepless agony.

She married Hemingway, and was helping to support him because she believed in his talent as a writer: a real writer, not merely the youngest reporter on international matters during a critical time in Europe. How could she tell her husband the news? Would he be able to forgive her? How could she forgive herself?

The lost valise has provided material for several novels, including Joe Haldeman's *The Hemingway Hoax* (1990) and Paula McClain's *The Paris Wife* (2011), and has generally been regarded as a crucial event leading to Ernest and Hadley's breakup and divorce in 1927. "It can't be denied that the loss of the manuscripts was the beginning of the end for Hadley and Ernest," Gioia Diliberto observed in her first-rate biography, *Hadley* (1992):

> *The perfection of the marriage was tainted by the loss, and things were never quite the same again. Hadley felt guilty about the incident for the rest of her life. Even as an old woman, she couldn't talk about it without crying. Ernest never truly forgave her, and perhaps in his own mind, he used his lingering resentment to justify betraying her with another woman.*

The issue of betrayal would trouble Hemingway's four marriages, as he successively cast off one wife for another. Hadley understood from the beginning the danger posed by Ernest's attractiveness and attraction to other women, and decided to take the risk anyway.

1

THE PARIS HUSBAND

How It Really Was Between Ernest and Hadley
Hemingway

A RELATIONSHIP WITH RIVALS

H adley Richardson and Ernest Hemingway met
in October 1920 at a party at his friend Y.K.
Smith's Chicago apartment. She had arrived from
St. Louis on the overnight train and was ready, at
nearly 29 years of age, to take charge of her life. For
most of that life, she'd been treated as an invalid. Her
mother—born Florence Wyman—was a strong-
willed feminist with an abhorrence of what she
perceived as the "abnormal, inordinate, and insane"
sexual activity required of most women.
"Occasional and rare" sex for procreation was all
right, though, and she and her husband James
Richardson produced four children. Hadley was the

5

youngest, and subjected to physical and psychological abuse in childhood. Her mother infantilized her, insisting that she stay in bed at the least hint of sniffles. Florence also dominated her husband, who suffered from drinking problems and financial difficulties. When Hadley was 13, he killed himself with a pistol shot to the head.

Hadley went to Mary Institute, the St. Louis girls' school founded by T.S. Eliot's grandfather. Although shy and reserved, she did well in her studies and made several lifelong friends. At the family's home in the fashionable West End, she practiced diligently on the *two* Steinway grand pianos in the music room, developing the musical talent she'd inherited from her mother. On a trip to Europe with her mother and sister Fonnie, the 17-year-old Hadley met the gifted piano teacher Anne Simon. Impressed by Hadley's playing, Simon encouraged her to drop out of Mary Institute and study piano in Washington, D.C. Hadley very much wanted to go, but her mother said no.

Instead, she finished her senior year and enrolled at Bryn Mawr College, perhaps the most rigorous of the Seven Sisters. There, presumably, Hadley could escape her mother's stifling domination. But college did not work for her. Soon after she started her studies, she was deeply affected by the accidental

6

death of her favorite sibling, Dorothea, 11 years her senior. At Bryn Mawr, she formed a close friendship with another student, and her mother (though a thousand miles away) became convinced that Hadley had entered into a lesbian relationship. That "rotten suggestion of evil" effectively ended the friendship and plunged Hadley into depression. Unable to concentrate on her work, she did poorly on her exams, withdrew from Bryn Mawr in May 1912, and limped home.

Back in St. Louis, her mother and sister Fonnie continued to treat Hadley as a frail creature unfit to lead an ordinary existence. For several years, her behavior seemed to justify that judgment: she languished around the house, reading, playing the piano, and doing little else. Yet when her mother fell ill, Hadley took over the caretaking duties for the family. After her mother died in August 1920, she felt empowered to strike out on her own.

What brought Hadley to Chicago two months later was a letter of invitation from Y.K. Smith's sister Katy. The two had been classmates at Mary Institute, and although Katy was a far more independent "new woman" than Hadley—she'd graduated from the University of Missouri and was pursuing a career as a journalist—they had kept in touch ever since. Y.K., a successful copywriter for an advertising firm, was Katy's older brother. He and his wife Doodles, a pianist, maintained an open marriage, a shocking arrangement at that time and in that place. They rented out rooms in their apartment house in Chicago's bohemian district to young men of promising talent, and threw lively parties there.

Undoubtedly, Katy thought that inviting Hadley to attend one of those parties would help liberate her from her repressive family background. But she could hardly have anticipated how well the evening would work out for her friend, or how badly for herself. That night, Katy learned a lesson that Hadley herself was to learn a few years later: the danger of introducing young Ernest Hemingway to an attractive friend.

Hemingway arrived at the party accompanied by Bill Smith, Katy's younger brother. Ernest had known the Smiths for years, for they were neighbors during the summers that both families spent in northern Michigan. Bill was a favorite fishing companion and close friend. As for Katy, although she, like Hadley, was eight years Ernest's senior—she'd seen him grow from a callow 10-year-old to a remarkably good-looking young man—she was now in love with him. And there could be no doubt that he cut a dashing figure: handsome, with dark hair, a wide grin, flashing brown eyes, and an

8

Italian officer's cape draped across his shoulders. Slim and tall, he bore little resemblance to the bearded and rugged Papa Hemingway of latter years. In photographs from that time, he looks rather like a young T.S. Eliot.

Ernest was drawn immediately to the new young woman from St. Louis. He liked Hadley's red hair, golden good looks, beautiful figure, and the dress she'd bought for the party. He liked her for the way she was, in Diliberto's description, "unpretentious, submissive, intelligent, sexy, tough in spirit." And they had a great deal in common too, as upper-middle-class Midwesterners with parallel backgrounds. Both had dominant mothers and deeply disturbed fathers; in fact, Ernest's father would kill himself in 1928, just as Hadley's had done in 1905. Both were eager to free themselves from unhealthy family situations. "The world's a jail, and we're going to break it together," Hadley wrote him soon after they met.

Both had artistic ambitions, too—Ernest as a writer and Hadley as a musician—but with the significant difference that once liberated from her confinement, Hadley devoted herself to *his* future. She believed in Ernest absolutely, and gave his writing her entire emotional and financial support.

Hadley stayed on in Chicago for three weeks after

the night of the party, and by the end of that time, she and Ernest were beginning to talk about marriage. Katy Smith was embittered at being cast aside for her former school friend. "You have no judgment," she told Hadley when she heard of their engagement. The comment struck home, as revealed in a letter Hadley wrote to Ernest. "The story of how you gyped Butstein [one of Katy's nicknames] makes me weak in the knees for my own future," she wrote. "I say it would be unscroopulous [sic] to work me that way."

Ernest declined to tell Hadley the details of his relationship with Katy, but he explored the romance in two unpublished sketches written before his marriage to Hadley in September 1921, as well as in "Summer People," a story printed posthumously in *The Nick Adams Stories* (1972). "Summer People" is set in northern Michigan and contains a scene depicting copulation between "Wemedge" (a nickname for Ernest) and "Stut" (another nickname for Katy). Katy, who married novelist John Dos Passos a decade later, denied that she and Ernest had ever been lovers.

The first of the unpublished pieces is written in the form of a letter (unsent) to Hadley. Ernest, his friend Bill Horne from the Red Cross ambulance service, and Katy ("Stut") are discussing his forthcoming marriage.

Stut says she thinks you oughta allow her to wear half mourning ... Said she'd try and remember it was your wedding ... Says she gives us a year at the longest—says you'll be off me inside of a year and that then she'll come over and live with us to hold the home together.

Bill Horne thought Ernest should delay getting married until he had resolved his relationship with Katy. Ernest passed on this advice in a letter to Hadley, admitting that he felt troubled about the matter. She was suitably alarmed, and responded that if a delay were necessary, it was all right with her. She was sure of her feelings and of the love they shared. And she wanted the same commitment from him. "I want you to think very hard about it all and make very sure that all's right for our marriage way, way inside."

In the second unpublished item, a story called "The Current," Ernest showed his awareness of Hadley's doubts about marrying him. In the story, a red-haired young woman named Dorothy Hadley refuses the proposal of her suitor on the grounds that he "could never be really in love with anyone."

Besides, he was too good-looking. She would not subject herself to going out with him and overhearing people say, "Who is that red-haired girl with that handsome man?"

Hadley decided to marry Ernest despite such reservations. But he did not make it easy for her to overcome these doubts. It soon became clear to her that she would always compete for his affection with others—women and men alike.

LIFE BEFORE HADLEY

Ernest had crushes on at least two girls at Oak Park high school—these documented for the first time by Robert K. Elder in 2016-17—but neither of these developed into a serious romantic relationship. That would not happen until he shipped off to Italy as an ambulance driver in the spring of 1918, and suffered two severe woundings. The first came around midnight on July 8, 1918, from Austrian mortar and machine gun fire. The second and more lasting wound was inflicted by Agnes von Kurowsky, the tall, attractive nurse he fell in love with while recuperating at the American Red Cross hospital in Milan. They made plans to be married, but after the armistice in November 1918, Ernest was shipped back to the States and Agnes (eight years his senior, like

Hadley) stayed in Italy to serve out her term as a Red Cross nurse.

In his absence, she formed a liaison with an Italian officer. The "Dear Ernest" letter she wrote him arrived in March 1919. She expected great things from him, she said, but she was simply too old for him, and she expected to marry her new lover (as it happened, she didn't). Ernest was devastated. He'd fallen deeply in love, and the rejection plunged him into the depths of depression. He emerged with a determination not to risk giving too much of himself to anyone ever again.

In the 18 months between Agnes's jilting and the party in Chicago where he met Hadley Richardson, Ernest had a series of relationships with women. One of these surely involved Katy Smith. The others were with younger girls he met in Horton Bay and Petoskey, Michigan, during the summer and fall of 1919: Irene Goldstein, a dark-haired beauty exactly his age; Marjorie Bump, a redhead two years younger; and Grace Quinlan, who was barely into her teens. But he made no commitments to them, and maintained the male friendships—mostly tied to fishing, the outdoors, and the war—that he could pursue without emotional consequences.

Marjorie Bump was probably the most important of the Michigan relationships. She and Ernest met in 1915, when—not quite 14 to his 16—she proudly showed him the speckled trout she'd just caught; they remained friends from that moment until his marriage. With her red hair and fetching freckles, she looked like a somewhat shorter version of Hadley.

If Hemingway's fiction is any guide, their romance ended through the intervention of Bill Smith. In "The End of Something" and "The Three-Day Blow," companion stories in Hemingway's first book, *In Our Time* (1925), a character modeled on Bill Smith (and called by that name in the first draft) congratulates Hemingway's avatar, Nick Adams, for breaking off with a young woman named Marjorie—presumably Marjorie Bump. "Once a man's married," Bill declares, "he's absolutely bitched ... done for." Nick wasn't so sure about that. Breaking off with Marge made him feel "as though everything was all gone to hell inside." As Hemingway scholar H. R. Stoneback commented in a revealing article about the real Marjorie Bump and these stories, what came to an end for Nick in "The End of Something" was his innocence. He was no longer a carefree young lad; he had to make choices, and he chose to discard Marge.

Yet at the end of "The Three-Day Blow," Nick still hopes to make it up with her: "Nothing was finished.

Nothing was ever lost. He would go into town on Saturday." In real life, Ernest stayed up north in the fall of 1919 and saw a great deal of Marjorie, then a senior at Petoskey High School en route to college at Washington University in St. Louis. During the summer at Horton Bay they'd taken moonlight swims and fished for rainbows, and in Petoskey, Ernest met Marge when school let out. He showed her the apprentice short stories he was writing, and they read and talked about books that the town librarian disapproved of, including Maurice Hewlett's *The Forest Lovers* (1898). That summer and fall, he later wrote her, were "idyllic—Perfect as some days in Spring are and mountain valleys you pass on puffing trains—and other impermanent things."

Irene Goldstein was another of Ernest's interests. She was the most beautiful woman in Petoskey, or so Hemingway—and others—thought. The granddaughter of the founder of the city's leading department store, she graduated from high school in 1917 and went on to Lake Forest College in Chicago's fashionable north suburbs and then to Columbia College of Expression and Physical Education in the city itself. Home from college during Christmas break in 1919, she partied with Ernest in Petoskey, and they dated in Chicago over the next month before Hemingway left town to write part-time for the *Toronto Star Weekly*.

Ernest was back at the family home on Walloon Lake, just outside Petoskey, during the summer of 1920, and he and Irene played a lot of tennis together—nearly every day for several weeks. As always with Hemingway, a strong atmosphere of competition prevailed. He "played very dramatically," she recalled, slamming his racket to the court when he missed an easy shot.

Theirs was hardly a love story, but they were attracted to each other and Ernest was reluctant to break the connection. It was *after* his three-week courtship of Hadley in the fall of 1920 that Ernest made physical overtures to Irene. In late December, he took her to Y.K. Smith's apartment in Chicago, and as they were about to leave—she was on her way to Grand Island, Nebraska, to teach physical education at a high school—he flung himself on her. "I don't do this," she protested. Ernest backed off and took her to the train station by taxicab.

That's what happened according to Irene's recollection. Ernest told a different story to Hadley. His letter to her about the incident has not survived, but it's possible to construe what he must have said from Hadley's answer. Irene got carried away by her emotions and had made a pass *at him*, Ernest claimed, but he had held her off. Hadley admired his resolve. "Best sort of person you are," she wrote him on January 8. "I love you."

Ernest and Irene continued their correspondence during the winter and spring of 1921. As Miami University of Ohio professor Donald Daiker has pointed out, these letters were more breezy than passionate. Yet it is significant that in a letter dated March 16, Ernest told Irene that he was moving to a new apartment in Chicago and that "if [she were] going to be here during July" he'd stick around, for she knew he was "fond of [her]." He said nothing about his engagement to Hadley.

Manifestly, Ernest liked pursuing (or, even better, being pursued by) two or more women at the same time. Not just women, but also young girls, as in the case of Grace Quinlan, the precocious 14-year-old to whom he wrote two letters a few weeks prior to his wedding. He addressed her as "Dearest G" in both letters, and in one of them told her he'd dreamed about her and hoped to see her in Petoskey before the day of "heavy marriage." (He also sent her photographs of himself and Hadley and asked her to recommend a minister—either Presbyterian or Episcopal—to perform the ceremony.) He sounded even more affectionate in the other letter. "I'm glad your the same very dear, very beautiful, very much older than your years, very unsatisfied (Thank Gawd) with Petoskey person that you are," he wrote, and signed off with "Good night old Dearest—I love you a very much." Were these love letters? It's difficult to say. Ernest switched gears immediately following his amorous remarks, identifying the relationship as that of a brother and sister. Grace was "the best of all sisters"; Ernest was "always your Bro."

Hemingway had grown up in a household full of females. His three closest siblings were girls: Marcelline, a year older, Ursula, three years younger, and Madelaine (Sunny), five years his junior. Ernest and his older sister were "twinned" by their mother, who dressed them the same during their early years. Both of them wore skirts when the family was in Oak Park, and both donned boys' attire when they went north for the summer months. Ernest felt closer to the two younger sisters, though, and closest of all to Ursula, who appears as a worshipful companion to him named "Littless" in the posthumously published story "The Last Good Country." He enjoyed being admired by them as bigger, bolder, and more assertive, and coveted that kind of adoration from others as well: from Grace Quinlan, up in Michigan, and later in life from the succession of younger women he called "Daughter."

Shortly after his 21st birthday in July 1920, Ernest and Ted Brumback, his friend from the *Kansas City Star*, stayed at Windemere, the Hemingway family house on Walloon Lake. One night the two men accompanied Ursula and Sunny—along with two other girls and two boys, all of them summer visitors—on a clandestine early hours picnic. The conspirators stole out at midnight, but the empty beds were discovered, and when the group paddled home at 3 a.m. a posse of outraged parents awaited them. This incident inspired Ernest's mother to order him off the premises. He was irresponsible, she told him in a devastating letter. He was thoughtless of others. He needed to grow up.

Unless you, my son Ernest, come to yourself; cease your lazy loafing and pleasure seeking; borrowing with no thought of returning; stop trying to graft a living off anybody and everybody; spending all your earnings lavishly and wastefully on luxuries for yourself; stop trading on your hansome [sic] face to fool little gullable [sic] girls, and neglecting your duties to God and your Savior, Jesus Christ; unless, in other words, you come into your manhood, there is nothing before you but bankruptcy.

Then, elaborating on the metaphor, she told him

he'd overdrawn on the bank account of her mother's love.

This was a dressing-down Ernest found hard to forgive. Like the jilting by Agnes von Kurowsky, it wounded his sense of himself, his *amour propre*. And besides, he already resented what he regarded as his mother's dominance of his father. He decided he would not let that happen to him. Better to be the loved one, the dominator, free to attract gullible little girls and mature women.

Not even his wedding could cure him of this neurosis. As he made preparations for the event, he insisted on inviting his Petoskey girls and Agnes as well.

The Hemingways' honeymoon was not auspicious. The newlyweds stayed at Windemere, and the neighbors kept telling Hadley "what a wonderful *young* man" she'd married. (He'd coached her to lie and say he was thirty when strangers asked about the difference in their ages.) One day he took her to the homes of Marjorie Bump and Grace Quinlan so that she could see for herself the women he rejected for her. Grace seemed terribly embarrassed by the visit. Though cockeyed in love, Hadley resented this exercise of male vanity. She was beginning to understand that her husband would always want other women around, and that she would inevitably be competing with rivals for her husband's affection.

Not all of them were female; his appeal transcended gender boundaries. During Ernest and Hadley's courtship period, two of his male friends encouraged him to put off the wedding indefinitely. Bill Smith argued against marriage on the grounds that it would end the fishing trips the two men enjoyed together and would probably be bad for his writing as well. Ernest passed on this news to Hadley, making her aware of an "entirely hostile camp" opposing their plans. Bill only wanted him "as a free-lance playmate," she wrote Ernest, and she wasn't buying Bill's supposedly "altruistic" worry about his writing. No one believed in him more than she did, and she would do everything possible to advance his career.

Jim Gamble posed a more complicated problem. A captain with the Red Cross, the wealthy American had befriended Hemingway during the war and drove him to Fossalta di Piave, Italy, where he was severely wounded in July 1918. Gamble visited Hemingway in the Milan hospital where he was recuperating—and falling in love with Agnes von Kurowsky. In October, Hemingway went back to the front, but he came down with jaundice almost immediately. Once again Gamble was there, driving him back to Milan to recover from his illness. He invited Ernest to spend part of the Christmas holiday with him in a villa he'd rented in Taormina, Sicily, and Hemingway accepted.

In a letter to E.E. (Chink) Dorman-Smith, an Anglo-Irish officer he'd met at the Officers' Club in Milan, Hemingway denied that he'd ever reached Taormina. He'd set out for that destination, he claimed, but was waylaid en route by his hostess in the first hotel where he stopped. She'd hidden his clothes and kept him to herself for a week. This was complete fiction; Hemingway and Gamble spent that week together in Taormina, and bonded there. By Christmas, the war had ended, and Gamble made the young ambulance driver an offer that was difficult to refuse: he asked Ernest to remain in Italy for a year as Gamble's secretary and companion, all expenses paid.

Agnes, however, scotched that plan, fearing it would turn Ernest into a bum, a sponger, a floater. She insisted he go back to the States with the understanding that she would follow and they would be married after her nursing duties were over. Hemingway did sail back on January 6, 1919, but stayed in touch with Gamble. On March 3, only days before the devastating breakup news from Agnes arrived, he wrote his former Red Cross captain rhapsodizing about their stay in Taormina. He mentioned their nighttime strolls, pleasantly "illuminated" through the beautiful Sicilian city, and the times they watched the moon reflecting on the sea below and Mount Etna fuming above. He yearned to be back there, and raised a glass in memory to Gamble, his "Chief."

By that time Gamble was in Philadelphia. When Hemingway's letter, which had been mailed overseas, finally reached him in mid-April, he responded immediately. Not a day had gone by when he had not thought of Ernest, he wrote. Italy was out for the time being, but he invited Hemingway to join him at his "place in the mountains" in Eagles Mere, Pennsylvania. Jim would paint, Ernest could bring his typewriter along (Jim had a few stories to suggest), and together they could enjoy the beauty of springtime, with "practically nobody" around to disturb them.

Still heartbroken over Agnes's jilting, Hemingway did not accept that invitation. He kept the door to their friendship open, however, and in December 1920, just as Ernest and Hadley were agreeing to an engagement, Gamble once more asked Hemingway to join him in Italy, this time for five months in Rome.

At first, Hemingway was inclined to accept this

offer. At the time, he was editing and writing most of the material for the *Cooperative Commonwealth* magazine. It was scut work at best and used up much of the energy he wanted to invest in his fiction, so Gamble's proposal sounded enticing to him.

Quite naturally, he wanted to get Hadley's reaction before making any kind of commitment. Ernest must have mentioned Gamble's offer before Hadley's December 20 letter, in which she remarked that "Jim Gamble sounds great if you like him so." Ernest replied three days later, apologizing for not being able to join her in St. Louis for a New Year's Eve party. He was broke, he explained, having spent too much on Christmas presents for his younger siblings, and he couldn't afford the trip. Then he added, by way of reassurance, that "Jim Gamble is great, and I love him a lot. But not like I love you."

The prospective journey to Rome came to a head with Gamble's cable and letter of December 27. Jim proposed that they sail on the *Rochambeau,* leaving New York on Tuesday, January 4, 1921, but he was prepared to adjust his plans to conform to Ernest's wishes. He also inquired about what had been going on in Ernest's life since they last communicated: "Married? Writing? Making money, or what?" He added that the trip would be inexpensive, with the Italian lira "only worth three cents."

In his cabled reply on the 27th, Ernest did not directly say yes or no. Here's how the wire read: "Rather go to Rome with you than Heaven. Stop." (Then, crossed out: "Not married.") "But am broke. Stop. Too sad for words. Stop. Writing and selling it. Stop." (Then, again, written on the side of the page and crossed out: "Unmarried.") "Don't get rich. All authors poor first then rich. Stop. Me no exception. Stop. Wouldn't we have a great time. Stop. Lord how I envy you." Signed "Hemmy."

In pleading poverty, Ernest may have been seeking further confirmation from Gamble about the exact financial arrangements. No record survives of Jim's response, but two days later, Ernest wrote Hadley that things were "all up in the air" and he was liable to leave Tuesday for five months of writing under ideal conditions in Rome. To help make ends meet, he could send articles to the *Cooperative Commonwealth* about the cooperative movement in Europe; the exchange rate of 30 lire to one dollar would make this a workable arrangement. Y.K. Smith, his landlord in Chicago, said Ernest would be "an utter damned fool" if he didn't go. His father favored it, too. What did Hadley think?

Hadley must have been distressed about the proposal, but she struck exactly the right notes in her comments about it. Earlier, she had written

Ernest that she would miss him "pretty frightfully" unless the five-month absence produced "a great gain" in his work. Still, she commented in her Christmas Day letter, "It might be just as much fun to write to you and hear from you in Rome as Chicago." But in her special delivery letter of December 31, in which she responded to a specific query about five months with an ocean between them, she wrote, "I hope you can tell me the reasons for and against Rome." So far, Ernest had emphasized the pros, ignoring the cons.

If he was still in doubt about whether to accept Gamble's offer, it may have been Hadley's report on New Year's Eve that settled the question. She went to the party with Dick Pierce, and told Ernest all about it. At the University Club "there was so much to drink you never saw the like," and wild dancing to a ragtime band. After midnight Dick and a few others came back to her house for more to drink, and she'd kissed him "in the quietest way." Suitably jealous, Hemingway wrote back that he was afraid of leaving her alone, and thereafter they began to talk of going to Italy *together*.

THE ROADS TO LAUSANNE

A year later, in December 1921, the newlyweds

embarked not for Rome but for Paris. They were armed with letters of introduction from novelist Sherwood Anderson to the American literati living there. Ernest arranged to send dispatches to the *Toronto Star* from Europe to help pay their way, but Hadley's trust fund provided most of the financial support. They spent very little on clothes and as little as possible on food and shelter. With the highly favorable exchange rate, they were able to travel around Europe extensively.

Once they'd gotten over their homesickness, which struck hard during their first Christmas overseas, the Hemingways were very happy together, and very much in love. Compatible in bed, they took turns playing the passive partner, "the little small petted one," as they called their role-playing. Then there were times when Ernest, who was something of a hypochondriac, required mothering for minor ills. Hadley filled that role as needed.

In addition to functioning as lover-wife-mother to Ernest, Hadley did an excellent job of being his pal. She eagerly adopted his sporting enthusiasms, for example, developing a knack for picking winners at the racetrack and becoming totally absorbed in the prizefights he took her to. Despite her supposed frailty, Hadley was quite athletic, and she mastered skiing easily; she also often beat Ernest on the tennis court. She drank along with him as well, matching his substantial capacity for liquor. In correspondence, Ernest celebrated Hadley ("Hash") and her accomplishments:

Hash and I have had and have a good time. We pastime the fights and the concerts, skiing, bullfights and the finnies. She fishes not with the usual feminine simulation of interest but like one of the men, she's as intelligent about fights as she is about music, she drinks like a male without remorse

Any marriage so ideal at the beginning runs the risk of deteriorating, and signs of discord began to emerge during the summer and fall of 1922. Ernest's remarkable appeal had something to do with it. So did exposure to the liberated sexual arrangements common among expatriates of that era. His absences to cover stories for the Toronto papers caused further friction. Also, Agnes von Kurowsky came back into the picture.

From the start, Hadley understood that Ernest was the dominant partner in the marriage, and she willingly accepted the situation. She thought of him as a paragon of physical attractiveness, the handsomest man she'd ever seen. "Even when he's asleep," she declared, "Ernest is beautiful." When

28

awake he radiated a strong personal magnetism. "He generated excitement," one of Hadley's friends from St. Louis commented, "because he was so intense about everything, about writing and boxing, about good food and drink. Everything we did took on new importance when he was with us." People were inevitably drawn to him. Men loved him. Women loved him. Children loved him. Even dogs loved him. "It was something," Hadley declared.

In Paris, Ernest and Hadley encountered relationships in the artistic community that would have shocked solid middle-class citizens back in the States. "A bisexual named McAlmon married a lesbian named Winifred who called herself Bryher," Michael Reynolds observed in the second volume of his magisterial Hemingway biography, *The Paris Years*. "As long as they remained married, McAlmon received a handsome allowance from Bryher's father. All the while, Bryher lived very quietly at Territet, Switzerland with Ezra [Pound's] old girl friend Hilda Doolittle, who had a child fathered perhaps by D.H. Lawrence."

At first, Ernest was disgusted by the gay men who inhabited the cafes of Paris, occasionally taking flight "like the birds to go off to Brussels or London or the Basque coast to return again even more like the birds." However, he grew more tolerant over time, even if his tolerance could be self-serving. He chose to ignore Robert McAlmon's bisexuality on the grounds that McAlmon did not parade his nature, showed real promise as a prose writer, and, with his father-in-law's money, started the small press that published Hemingway's first book, *Three Stories and Ten Poems* (1923). With Hemingway's developing broadmindedness on such issues came an erosion of the Oak Park values he had grown up with. In different ways, the two most important literary mentors he came to know in Paris, Gertrude Stein and Ezra Pound, also contributed to the relaxation—or at least widening—of his values.

It was Pound he met first, early in 1923, and the two men immediately became friends. They boxed and played tennis together, and in long conversations Pound expounded his theories about writing. With his shock of red hair—even redder than Hadley's—the flamboyant poet spoke as a master of the craft; after all, he'd vetted T.S. Eliot's *The Waste Land*. He counseled Hemingway to condense his flow of language and preached the benefits of understatement and irony. Less was more, in literature as in art and architecture.

LIFE AS AN EXPATRIATE

Pound also provided Ernest with an example of how a writer's marriage might be conducted. He was married to Dorothy Shakespear, a lovely blond Englishwoman whose mother had been William Butler Yeats's mistress. Both she and Hadley subordinated their own artistic drives—Dorothy's in painting, Hadley's in music—to those of their husbands. And both had trust funds to support their husbands' efforts. Where the bedroom was concerned, however, they diverged radically.

Ezra and Dorothy had an open marriage—and were entirely forthcoming about it. He had a series of affairs, with her consent. She wasn't much interested in sex, but he believed that his creative genius could only flower when stimulated by more than one woman. Henry (Mike) Strater, an American expatriate in Paris who painted two portraits of Hemingway in the spring of 1923, felt the same way. He too was regularly adulterous, justifying his behavior on the grounds that "all men of genius" led "old-fashioned immoral" lives. Hemingway should do the same, Strater recommended. Genius didn't *excuse* such behavior, he maintained; genius *required* it. Such male entitlement ran rampant in Hemingway's circle.

When McAlmon wrote his memoir of the period, he called it *Being Geniuses Together*.

Ernest didn't entirely agree with this philosophy, but exposure to it helped pave the path to a future breakup of his marriage. He remained faithful to Hadley, he told Bill Smith, because he was in love with her. If he were married but not in love, he'd feel free to sleep with anyone he pleased. And if he were in love with two women at the same time ... ?

As for Gertrude Stein, their friendship was not to last, but at the beginning, Ernest happily sat at her feet. The letter of introduction from Sherwood Anderson elicited an invitation to tea in March 1922, and Ernest and Hadley duly presented themselves at 27 rue de Fleurus, where Stein and her partner Alice B. Toklas kept house and a well-known literary salon. Thin, dark, and sharp-nosed, Toklas at once ushered Hadley to a far corner of the room so that Stein, Buddha-like in appearance and girth, could hold forth with her husband, the young man whose promise Anderson had testified to. Hemingway was enormously impressed by Stein. She was always right about writing, he thought.

But Stein was a tough editor. "There is a great deal of description in this," she said of the fragmentary novel Ernest was working on in 1922, "and not particularly good description. Begin over again and concentrate." Not exactly the words he wanted to hear.

Perhaps her most important piece of advice was that Hemingway had to give up journalism if he wanted to succeed as a writer. Specifically, she warned him that sticking solely to the facts—a necessity in newspaper reporting—might weaken his powers of invention. Also, in fiction, he couldn't rely on timeliness to generate reader interest. He took those lessons to heart, and reconfigured them in a 1935 article about the difference between reporting and fiction. "When you describe something that has happened that day the timeliness makes people see it in their own imaginations," he wrote. A month later, though, the relevance was gone and no one would remember the newspaper account. "But if you make it up instead of describing it you can make it round and whole and solid and give it life."

Useful as Stein's advice proved to be, Hemingway was not yet ready to abandon journalism. Hadley provided the bulk of the income they needed to live in reasonable comfort overseas, but he was determined to make as much as he could on his own. Besides, though barely of voting age, he had wangled a dream job as a foreign correspondent sending dispatches to the Toronto papers, both the *Daily Star* and the more feature-oriented *Star Weekly*. The space-rates pay for his pieces was only adequate, but the papers also paid salary and expenses when he was on assignment. On that basis, Hemingway went to Italy to report on the Conference in Genoa, an international economic forum held in April 1922; to Constantinople for the end of the Greco-Turkish War in October; and to Lausanne for the peace talks in November and December.

On these assignments, Ernest had the opportunity to meet and learn from some of the most prominent newsmen of the time, among them Lincoln Steffens and William Bolitho Ryall, figures as influential in establishing his worldview—his *Weltanschauung*—as Stein and Pound were in developing his writing. Almost everyone who met him during those early expatriate years came away believing in his future. This was due in part to his charismatic presence, but also to his dedication to the task at hand. Ernest worked hard at his journalism as well as his fiction. He "was gay, he was sentimental," Steffens remembered, "but he was always at work."

All that traveling around Europe was highly educational for Ernest, who had never gone to college. But Hadley objected to his repeated trips. They took her husband away from home for weeks at a time, and eventually led to their first serious marital dispute.

Ernest spent nearly a month in Genoa, during which he mailed or cabled 23 articles back to Toronto. Most were anecdotal pieces. The 22-year-old reporter was a quick study, but where issues were concerned, he affected an authority that he had not earned. No matter: the Toronto papers wanted color, and he supplied it. Candid glimpses of the great men of the day enlivened his copy. Chancellor Joseph Wirth of Germany looked like a tuba player in an oompah-pah band, he reported, and Jean-Louis Barthou, leader of the French delegation at the conference, resembled the left-hand Smith brother on the famous cough drop box. Given his youthful appearance, Prime Minister David Lloyd George of England was described as "a boy subaltern just out of Sandhurst."

John Bone, his boss in Toronto, was pleased with the work. The paper gave prominent play to his articles and paid him well enough to finance an extensive trip in the summer of 1922 that he and Hadley took together. They began at the Gangwisch pension in Chamby-sur-Montreux, Switzerland, where the amiable Chink Dorman-Smith joined them for some fishing and mountain climbing. From there the three of them hiked over the Great St.

Bernard Pass into Italy. It was a tough trip for Hadley, who gamely tried to keep pace despite not having proper hiking boots for the heavy snow. She and Ernest stayed in Aosta a few days while she recovered from swollen legs and blistered feet.

After Chink left to rejoin his unit in Cologne, the couple embarked on the Italian tour Ernest had long been planning. He wanted to revisit the sites of his wartime service and to show them to Hadley. In Milan, this meant the building on the Via Manzoni that had served as the Red Cross hospital and the massive Duomo. In Schio, he showed her his first post in Italy, which he remembered as "one of the finest places on earth," and the Due Spadi hotel. In Fossalta di Piave, he took her to where he had been wounded. The Hemingways saw it all, but nothing was the same. The weather was rainy, the Due Spadi had become "a small mean inn," and in Fossalta, where thousands had died, he couldn't find any sign of the war beyond a single rusty shell fragment. "[D]ont ever go back," he wrote Bill Horne, "because it is all gone and Italy is all gone." Chasing yesterdays was "a bum show."

Ernest and Hadley took another trip later that summer, this time to the Black Forest in Germany. They traveled with two other American couples: Bill and Sally Bird, and Lewis Galantière and his fiancée

Dorothy Butler. Hemingway had become friendly with Bill Bird, who was in charge of the Continental branch of the Consolidated Press, when they were covering the conference in Genoa. Galantière, a friend of Sherwood Anderson's, took the Hemingways out to dinner and helped them find a place to live soon after their arrival in Paris. The six expatriates hiked through the forest, fishing for trout and staying in inns that had become so inexpensive because of German inflation that, as Ernest wrote to Gertrude Stein, "we can't afford to leave this country."

It would have been a perfect trip were it not for both Hemingways' dislike of Dorothy Butler. She was selfish and demanding, they thought, and when everyone was back in Paris Ernest told Dorothy so in one of his occasional brutal letters (not all were sent). Lewis would be better off without her, he wrote. He'd made an effort to like her in hopes of seeing Lewis occasionally, but "even though I kissed you, Dorothy, even while I kissed you, I never liked you." As Hadley remarked, Ernest was "a good hater," with some of his nastiest animus directed toward women who dominated their mates.

That was usually not a problem with Hadley, but she did rebel when—shortly after the Black Forest sojourn—Ernest took on another assignment for the

Toronto Star, this time to cover the last phase of the Greco-Turkish War. The Turks were clearly winning. On September 15, Kemal Pasha's troops burned Smyrna, leaving 60,000 Greeks and Armenians homeless, and they continued their advance toward Constantinople, then under Allied protection. Wanting desperately to be on the scene, Hemingway cabled John Bone: "WONDERFUL ASSIGNMENT BUT IF WAR HASTE NECESSARY STOP IF NO WAR GREAT SERIES NEAR EAST ARTICLES ANYWAY." On September 20, Bone sent him $500 to take care of expenses, and Hemingway set about securing visas, working out the details of a secret deal with Frank Mason of the International News Service (INS), and trying to persuade Hadley that he really had to go to Constantinople.

Genoa had been bad enough, Hadley thought, but Constantinople was a lot further away and considerably more dangerous. Fighting was still going on, the Allies were considering joining the war to halt the Turkish advance, and rumors were circulating about epidemics. Hadley didn't want her husband risking his life there. She didn't fancy being left alone in Paris for a month or more. And she balked at Ernest's arrangement with INS.

Hemingway was supposed to be under exclusive

contract with the *Toronto Star*. On the side, though, he agreed to supply INS with spot news stories under the byline of John Hadley. It's not clear how much Mason agreed to pay for these dispatches or whether they included only space rates or salary and expenses as well. In any case, it was double-dipping, and it "seared [Hadley's] Puritan soul." She put her foot down, or tried to. For three long days they slept and ate side by side, but Hadley refused to speak to him. "It was just awful," she recalled in retrospect, characteristically taking most of the blame for interfering with Ernest's profession.

The quarrel had its effects. On September 24, the night before he left, Hemingway and Lincoln Steffens watched the fight where the French-Senegalese boxer Battling Siki "nearly kill[ed] [Georges] Carpentier." The next day, still without a word between Hadley and himself, Ernest left for Constantinople.

While he was there, Ernest sent hard news by cable to the *Star's* London office under his own byline—and cabled similar reports to Mason, for the INS wire, from "John Hadley." Hemingway and Mason may have thought they could get away with this maneuver because INS had no outlets in Canada. But Bone read the U.S. papers as well, where he found pieces closely resembling the ones he was paying for. On October 6, Bone objected with a wire to Hemingway: "SPOT NEWS DUPLICATING SERVICES [the wire services, that is, and INS in particular] WANT SPECIAL INTERVIEWS COLD." That gave Ernest pause. When he got back to Paris and sent in his expense account, he'd have to find a way of justifying himself to Bone.

Meanwhile, Hemingway was struggling physically. He came down with malaria and was sick for most of the month he was away. Somehow he managed to produce enough lively features—some of them mailed rather than cabled to save costs—to satisfy Toronto. "Constantinople is noisy, hot, hilly, dirty, and beautiful," he began his first dispatch. And also hazardous: British troops had arrived to head off an invasion by the Turks, and all the foreigners were frightened, suffering "the sickening, cold, crawling fear-thrill" of those who could not get away.

Near Adrianople, Hemingway witnessed firsthand the collateral damage of the war: 20 miles of carts jamming the road to Karagatch, with thousands of Greek refugees slogging along beside them through the rain. In one of the carts, a woman was groaning in labor, her small daughter crying as she watched. Ernest wrote a piece describing the scene; it was the best work of his assignment. His revised version, later included as one of the interchapters for *In Our Time* (1925), was even better. He remained in bad shape himself, though, taking quinine and aspirin for the lingering malaria, his head shaved to keep lice at bay. More than ready to come home, he cabled the refugee story and began the long trip back.

He arrived in Paris on the morning of October 25, a month to the day since he left, and was reunited with Hadley. On the journey through Bulgaria, Serbia, Yugoslavia, and Italy, Ernest had been wondering what to expect, since they'd parted on such unpleasant terms and only three of her letters had reached him. He brought peace offerings with him, including an amber necklace he'd bought from a white Russian reduced to waiting tables in Constantinople. Hadley kept the necklace all her life, but gifts were hardly necessary. Remorseful about the silent treatment she'd subjected Ernest to, Hadley was ecstatic to see him again. He came back to her exhausted, feverish and feeling sorry for himself, and she took her usual "great great care of him" during his nearly week-long recovery.

The protective mothering did its job. Ernest emerged "on top of the wave, absolutely roistering with the most wonderful joyousness." He and

Hadley were as happy as they'd ever been, and Ernest rhapsodized about it in a letter to Bill Horne:

> *[Hadley] was more beautiful than ever and we loved each other very much and went everywhere together, the races at Auteuil with every body crowded around the big charcoal braziers and a November bright blue sky and the turf hard and the fields good and we watching every race from the top of the stands.*

That was the way Hadley wanted it, going "everywhere together" with Ernest. By the end of November, however, they would be separated once again.

THE CONFERENCE, THE VALISE, AND WHAT WAS LOST

As the first order of business when he returned from the Near East, Hemingway tried to clear the air with John Bone. On October 27, he mailed his editor a long list of expenses, which in his calculations amounted to 300 francs (about $35) *less* than the $500 advance Bone had originally sent him. He duly enclosed a check covering the difference, presumably in an attempt to make amends for his duplicity with INS. Yet he also fabricated for Bone's benefit a cock-and-bull story about how one (only one, in his account) of his dispatches to the *Star* had turned up, nearly verbatim, on the INS news wire.

According to Hemingway, he was stuck in Adrianople with "what looked like a great story" on his hands. But because he was short on funds and had no way to pay the cable charges, he had it sent "Receiver to Pay to Frank Mason of the International News Service Paris" with instructions to relay it to the *Star*'s office in London. That much, at least, accurately reflected his arrangement with INS. What followed was pure invention, with Mason cast in the role of villain.

Mason promptly relayed the cable to London, Ernest claimed, but in addition "proceeded to steal and re-write as much of it as [he] could get away with." INS had thus "pirated" his work. He should not have placed so much confidence in Mason's honesty, Hemingway confessed sadly, and he'd had this "question of ethics" out with him.

Bone, a veteran in the field, probably regarded this explanation with skepticism. He liked Hemingway's writing, and wanted him to return to Toronto as a regular staffer, but must have wondered about his truthfulness. He duly paid Hemingway five weeks' salary at $75 a week, a windfall for Ernest and Hadley. He did not, however, assign his correspondent to cover the peace conference convening in Lausanne. All the statesmen in Europe would be there, and everyone in the press community in Paris was going, including Lincoln Steffens, Bill Bird, and Ernest's pal Guy Hickok, from the *Brooklyn Eagle*.

At the last minute, when no cable came from Toronto, Ernest made his own arrangements. Once again, he agreed to supply copy to Mason under the byline "John Hadley, International News Service Staff Correspondent," but this time he was on a salary-and-expenses basis. He also made a deal with Charles Bertelli, the Universal News Service's bureau chief in Paris, to file dispatches from Lausanne. Whatever Hemingway sent to INS probably went to Universal automatically, since both agencies were owned by Hearst. In the extensive back-and-forth exchanges between Hemingway and Mason during the conference, though, there is no mention of Universal or Bertelli.

The facts remain hazy at best, clouded after nearly a century. It is certain, however, that in Lausanne, as in Constantinople, Hemingway was supposed to be under exclusive contract to the Toronto papers. His arrangement with INS violated that provision, as did his deal with Universal. But at least in Lausanne, he was not charging the *Star* and INS for the same material. He sold only two features from Lausanne to the Toronto papers, both of them written and published after the conference ended.

Ernest knew he was engaging in dubious practices and subsequently admitted as much. "I was covering the Lausanne Conference for Hearst under the name of John Hadley," he wrote Bill Smith in 1924. "Was in the Near East for them too under the same name. Couldnt use my own on acct contract with the Star." Many years later, he contended that the whole irregular business was "covered by the statute of limitations."

Hemingway passed through Swiss customs on November 21, the day after the peace conference opened. Oddly, he carried with him two press cards: Frank Mason's and that of Guglielmo Emanuel, an Italian journalist and INS staff correspondent.

Initially, Hadley had planned to accompany her husband on his assignment. She could shop a little, take a holiday, and pay a visit to Chamby, where they were going to spend Christmas. Instead, she came down with a nasty cold and stayed in Paris. As she fought off her illness, Hadley wondered whether Ernest really wanted her to join him. He did his best to reassure her in his cables and a letter couched in their private baby talk:

[Cable] 24 November: POOR DEAR WICKEY STOP ANXIEST HAVE YOU COME SORRY BUM LETTER WASN'T MEANT BE STOP WIRE WHEN ARRIVE WEATHER GORGEOUS STEFF *[Lincoln Steffens]* SENDS LOVE STOP LOVE POO.

[Cable] 25 November: SORRIEST SICK HUSTLE DOWN HERE SOONS WELL ENOUGH FEEL TRAVELLY LOVE WICKY LOTSA SUN GOOD CLIMATE STOP IF REALLY SICK ADVISE INSTANTLY AS GLAD CHANCE COME HOME POO.

[Letter] 28 November: Poor dear little Wicky Poo, I'm so sorry you've felt so frightfully rotten and sick [not to be outdone, he followed this with an account of his own battle coughing up green stuff with black specks]. Certainly has been bad for us little tinies....

I've been crazy for you to come and would love so still but if you say you are too miserable for the trip you know what. But please Wickey realise that I want you and wasn't trying to stall...

Everybody sends you love. Steffens wrote you a letter. I love you dearest Wicky ... Anyhow both being laid out with colds we haven't lost so much time on the time of the month [a reference to the instances when they didn't have to take precautions against pregnancy] ... I do so hate for you to miss what is the most comfortable and jolly time for mums. Won't we sleep together though?... Dear sweet feather kitty with the castorated oil and the thowing up, I think it is so pitiful I could just cry.

I'm just your little wax puppy.

Love Pups to mups —

Ernest's duties in Lausanne proved more taxing than he anticipated. Appealing for Hadley's sympathy, he spelled out his grievances in excruciating detail. On a typical day, he never got around to lunch

till way after two and dinner always leftovers and the three places I have to go back and forth between are about 3 kilometers apart up and down hill and your always afraid you're missing something at one place or the other and they all talk French and the Russians are miles out of the way and I'm only a little tiny wax puppy. Mason has kiked me so much on money that I can't afford taxi's and have to take the street car and walk. And they expect me to cover them until midnight every night starting at nine in the morning.

"Everyone else has two men or an assistant," he went on, and covering all the breaking stories was "almost impossible cause they happen at the same time and far apart and everything ... Unless Mason gives me a lot of money I'll upgive the job some time this week and if he does give me money you've got to come here sick well or anything."

On Tuesday, November 28, the day before he wrote this letter, Mason and Hemingway exchanged cables addressing the issues of coverage at all hours and what INS was willing to pay for. Hemingway had missed an important story: the announcement by British Foreign Minister George Curzon that he supported an "open door policy" allowing all nations access to the Dardanelles—a policy that was anathema to the Russians and threatened to break up the conference. The INS office in New York complained to Mason that they'd been scooped, and told him to pass on the complaint to their man Hadley in Lausanne. Semi-furious, Hemingway drafted the following cable in reply:

Story Broke Eleven 23 Oclock if you want 24 hour service pay for it.

Then he crossed out that version and tried again:

Story Broke 22.30 Oclock
Twenty four hour service costly.

Mason got the message, and Hemingway got the raise he was angling for, from $60 to $95 a week. This exchange did not end their disputes over money, however. On December 14, as Ernest was preparing to leave the job and go to Chamby, he wired Mason asking for a payment of 800 Swiss francs to cover his expenses. He needed the money by Saturday the 16th to pay his hotel bill. Mason wired back that the INS books showed "approximately 500 Swiss francs" in expenses were due, and he asked Hemingway to rush his receipts for final payment. The next day, Hemingway responded with a classic example of cable humor:

SUGGEST   YOU   UPSTICK   BOOKS
ASSWARDS

In a letter to Mason on the same day, he expanded on his outrage. "There seems no possible way to regard your refusal to forward the money to me," he wrote, "except as a belief on your part that I was planning or t[r]ying to gyp you in some way." Whatever could have made Mason think that?

In his rare free moments in Lausanne, Hemingway

listened, rapt, as William Bolitho Ryall (who wrote for the *Manchester Guardian* under the pen name William Bolitho) discoursed on "the malady of power"—the way in which political dignitaries came to believe only in themselves while distrusting everyone else. Caustic and brilliant, the South African-born Ryall "told [him] things that were the beginning of [his] education in international politics," Hemingway later said. Ryall had a gift for debunking those in authority that suited Ernest's own proclivities; one of his first articles for the *Toronto Star*, back in 1920, made satirical sport of the city's mayor.

Under Ryall's guidance, Hemingway changed his mind about Benito Mussolini. Six months earlier he'd interviewed Mussolini in Milan, and the ensuing feature for the *Star* presented the Fascist leader in a favorable light. "Mussolini was a great surprise," Hemingway told his readers, not at all "the monster" he had been cast as but something of an intellectual, a big, brown-faced man with a slow smile who fondled the ears of a wolfhound puppy as they spoke.

That piece ran on June 24, 1922. On January 27, 1923, Ernest once again profiled Mussolini for the *Star*, but this time as "the biggest bluff in Europe," a theatrical character with no substance. As evidence,

Hemingway cited an anecdote from the press conference Mussolini held in Lausanne that seems almost too good to be true. The Italian leader was deep in concentration, reading a book, as 200 correspondents crowded into the room. Hemingway "tiptoed over behind him" to see what Mussolini was reading with such deep interest: "It was a French-English dictionary—held upside down."

The topics of clothing and sexual inclinations figured prominently in Ryall's gossip about the statesmen of Europe, and his opinions found their way into Hemingway's reports on the Lausanne conference and its luminaries. Take Mussolini's attire, for instance. Hemingway: "There is something wrong, even histrionically, with a man who wears white spats with a black shirt." Bolitho (Ryall's pseudonym): "We will never have Fascism in England; no Englishman will dress up, not even for a revolution."

Another object of analysis was Russian Foreign Minister Georgy Chicherin, who had impressed Hemingway at the Genoa conference by his "almost inhuman capacity for work." In Lausanne, the physically unimpressive Chicherin was photographed wearing a gaudy military uniform even though he had never served in any army. According to Ryall, this was because Chicherin's mother dressed him as a girl until he was 12; Hemingway wrote this theory into his dispatch on the Minister as if it were fact. "The boy who was kept in dresses until he was twelve years old always wanted to be a soldier. And soldiers make empires and empires make wars." Ryall's speculation resonated with Hemingway, whose own mother dressed him in girl's clothes when he was a boy.

The Treaty of Lausanne was signed, finally, in July 1923. It has been characterized as "the most successful and lasting peace settlement of the post-First World War period," which brought to an end "four years of strife and tension in the Near East." To Hemingway—as influenced by Ryall—it seemed more like a farce. Shortly after leaving Lausanne, he wrote a deeply cynical poem called "They All Made Peace—What Is Peace?"

Lord Curzon likes young boys.
So does Chicherin.
So does Mustapha Kemal. He is good looking too.
His eyes are too close together but he makes war.
That is the way he is.

Lord Curzon does not love Chicherin. Not at all.
His beard trickles and his hands are cold. He thinks
all the time.

Lord Curzon thinks too. But he is much taller and goes to Saint Moritz.

Mr. Child [American delegate Richard Child] does not wear a hat.

....

Mrs. Child has flat breasts and Mr. Child is an idealist and wrote Harding's campaign speeches and calls Senator
Beveridge Al.
You know me Al.
Lincoln Steffens is with Child. The big C. makes the joke easy.

Steffens had become a firm believer in Hemingway's future. The young writer really "dawned on me one night at the Lausanne peace conference," Steffens recalled in his autobiography. Ernest had brought along some of his cables from the Near East and his racetrack story, "My Old Man," for Steffens to read. Steffens was blown away by the cable about the Greek refugees, describing it as "a short but vivid, detailed picture of what he had seen in that miserable stream of hungry, frightened, uprooted people." The dispatch Steffens admired was improved when Hemingway rewrote it for book publication, reducing the number of adjectives from

30 to 10 and removing himself from the piece entirely, refusing to guide the reader's response. Steffens also liked "My Old Man" and sent it to a magazine editor in New York with his recommendation.

"Hemingway's was the surest future over there," Steffens decided. "He could, he would, do it some day." The confidence of the 56-year-old famous former muckraker meant a great deal to the 23-year-old Hemingway, who had published almost nothing beyond newspaper articles. Ernest spoke openly to Steffens about his private life, telling him about his experiences in the war and the nurse he'd planned to marry. If Agnes von Kurowsky were to come back into his life, he confessed, he might have to leave Hadley. At some time during November, he wrote Agnes a letter.

The exact contents of the letter aren't known, but we can intuit much of Ernest's message from her reply. He brought Agnes up to date on what had happened during the three years since she broke their engagement. He was married to Hadley, a fine musician who shared his love of the outdoors. He was traveling around Europe, as Agnes had longed to do, as a foreign correspondent for INS and the *Toronto Star*. He was living in Paris, a city Agnes loved. He was in contact with some of the leading writers and journalists of the time. His first book was to be published soon. In other words, did she realize what she had missed?

If Ernest was contemplating a reunion with Agnes, the letter she sent on December 22 was less than encouraging. After she recovered from the shock of hearing from him, she wrote, "I never was more pleased over anything in my life." She understood his bitterness over the way their "comradeship" ended, for she herself felt ready to break "somebody or something" when her Italian fiancé jilted her. She was not surprised to hear about his impending success, for she'd always known that he "would stand out from the background." How proud she would be "some day in the not-very-distant future to say 'Oh yes, Ernest Hemingway—Used to know him well during the war.'"

All of that was agreeable enough, even flattering, but there was no hint of resuming their romance. On the contrary, Agnes made a point of observing that their breakup had turned out for the best; Ernest must surely realize this now that he was married. Apparently, he hadn't mentioned that Hadley was actually a few months older than her, because Agnes reiterated her conviction that she was simply too old for him, just as she'd previously insisted in her "Dear Ernest" letter. She hoped that they could be good friends again, for friends were "great things to have." In closing, she offered him a firm handclasp, and signed off with "best wishes to you & Hadley ... Your old buddy Von (oh excuse me, it's Ag.)"

Eventually, Ernest must have concluded that no matter what he achieved, he could not change Agnes's feelings about him. Six months later, he finished "A Very Short Story," a fictional rendering of their romance and its end. In it, he changed her name from "Ag" to (excuse me) "Luz" and made her very much the villain of the piece for betraying his love.

He was still weighing the relationship 12 years later. In the famous story "The Snows of Kilimanjaro," he conjured up another version of how he felt about Agnes in 1922. The protagonist, a writer, is dying of jaundice on an African safari, and flashes back in memory to the time he'd gone to Constantinople, recalling "how he'd written her, the first one, the one who left him, a letter telling her he'd never been able to kill it ... How every one he had slept with had only made him miss her more. How what she had done could never matter since he knew he could not cure himself of loving her." The protagonist wrote this letter "cold sober" and asked his ex-lover to reply to his office in Paris, but the office forwarded the mail to his flat. The morning when he saw the handwriting "he went cold all over and tried to slip the letter underneath another. But his wife said, 'Who is that letter from, dear?' and that was the end of the beginning of that."

That was (mostly) fiction. Yet Ernest did write to Agnes, "the first one, the one who left him" in November 1922, though with less passion than his fictional writer conveyed, and she did write him back, offering in return no more than a virtual handshake. The passage from "The Snows of Kilimanjaro" seems to have convinced the public that Hadley knew about Ernest's letter. In *The Paris Wife*, Paula McLain invented a scene in which Ernest more or less asked Hadley's permission to write to Agnes, and one of his biographers depicts Ernest telling his wife when Agnes's reply arrived. But there is no evidence that Hadley knew anything about her husband's overture, or Agnes's answer. The exchange was Ernest's secret, something that would always lie between them, unspoken.

As would his reaction to the lost valise.

A lot of misinformation has been circulated about the valise and what Ernest did when he learned that the serious writing he'd been sweating over in Paris, the vignettes and stories he really cared about, had gone missing. Much of that misinformation came from Hemingway himself. In his writing, there is no reliable boundary between fact and fiction, and that's the way he wanted it. He was particularly annoyed when critics accused him of simply converting his own experiences into stories and novels. "I write some stories absolutely as they happen," he wrote to his editor Maxwell Perkins in 1933, while others he invented completely, and nobody could tell which was which.

Even in writing that purported to tell the truth, such as nonfiction articles, memoirs, and letters, Hemingway often let his imagination color the facts. In *A Moveable Feast* (1964), his posthumously published memoir of the Paris years he wrote during the 1950s, he set down his version of the stolen valise incident. The book's preface explicitly warns readers to expect occasional reordering or altering of what actually happened, yet nearly all Hemingway biographers have taken the account in the book as gospel. It was not.

Fact. What do we know for sure? Hadley arrived in Lausanne on the morning of December 3, distraught about losing her husband's literary work. Ernest was at the train station to meet her, accompanied by Lincoln Steffens. "She cried and cried and could not tell" him what was wrong, Hemingway remembered;

finally she told him about losing the valise and the stories and poems it contained. He'd "never seen anyone hurt by a thing other than death or unbearable suffering except Hadley when she told me about the things being gone." Steffens could also see how much she was suffering.

Fiction. What we think we know derives mostly from what Hemingway set down for posterity in *A Moveable Feast.* That he could not believe Hadley put *all* of his writing—handwritten originals, typed copies, and carbons—in the valise. That in desperate hope of finding some of this material, he left Hadley in Lausanne, "hired someone" to cover for him with INS, and took the next train back to Paris. That he found nothing: "It was true all right and I remember what I did in the night after I let myself into the flat and found it was true." That the next day he had lunch with Stein and Toklas, and then went back to Lausanne.

So Hemingway told us, but none of it was true. Ernest did not go directly to Paris after hearing the news—he waited until late January. He did not have a restorative lunch with Stein and Toklas, who were then in Saint-Rémy-de-Provence. Nor did he write the satirical poem "They All Made Peace" on the train ride back to Lausanne, as he told Edmund Wilson in an epistolary falsehood.

There were enough clues to Hemingway's inventions in *A Moveable Feast*, particularly in its lack of specificity. Who was the vague "someone" he hired to cover for him with INS? What unmentionable alcoholic and/or sexual sins did he commit during that night in Paris? Yet among Hemingway's numerous biographers, only James Mellow has resisted the temptation to repeat his yarn. Mellow was also Gertrude Stein's biographer, and he knew for certain that she couldn't have seen Hemingway (or anyone else) in Paris in December 1922.

A HUGE LOSS

Instead of going to Paris himself, Ernest asked a committee of three—Steffens, Hickok, and Bird—to look through the lost property office at the Gare de Lyon and to explore the possibility of offering a reward for the return of the valise. The search at the train station turned up nothing, Steffens reported in a letter dated December 9. As for the reward,

> [Bird] suggested advertising, but he said that would cost a couple of hundred francs and would get us no where unless we offered a big reward. We didn't feel that you would spend so much and your letter to Billy

*[Bird], received today, shows that you think only of
150 francs reward [less than one day's pay from INS].
No use, I think, and Billy said so. He would have to
get somebody that wrote French well to do the free ad
you asked for. More expense.*

If Ernest really wanted to pursue the ad-and-reward
plan, Steffens added, he should specify, via wire,
whether he wished "to spend what it would
evidently cost to induce the thief to take a chance
and bring back what you want and he doesn't."

The bottom line, as they both knew, was that the
thief undoubtedly valued only the valise itself and
had disposed of its written—and potentially
incriminating—contents. As Steffens concluded,
"I'm afraid the stuff is lost, Hem."

The measly 150-franc reward aside, it is clear that
both Ernest and Hadley were deeply hurt by the loss.
Ernest had been "very brave" when she delivered
the news, Hadley recalled, but she could see that
"his heart was broken." She'd caused him to suffer
an "irreparable loss." Something had happened that
could be neither forgotten nor undone, and their
marriage would never be the same. In a 1975
interview, when she was 83 years old, Hadley
radiated a glow as she reminisced about Ernest. But
when she was asked about losing his manuscripts,

she broke into tears. As Diliberto said in her biography (p.278), "[Hadley] sat there with tears on her face talking about it. She was right back there in Paris in 1922."

Ernest took it hard, too. "It was a bad time," he wrote in A *Moveable Feast*, "and I did not think I could write any more." The loss was so tremendous, he told Charles Fenton, that he "tried to forget it and put it out of his mind almost with surgery." For seven long weeks, during the winter sports and good fellowship at Chamby, he kept silent about the incident. "Never discuss casualties," his military friend Chink Dorman-Smith advised. Finally, though, he went back to Paris alone. On January 23, he unburdened himself to Ezra Pound.

"I suppose you heard about the loss of my Juvenilia?" he began. "I went to Paris last week to see what was left and found that Hadley had made the job complete by including all carbons, duplicates, etc." All that remained of his "complete works" were "three pencil drafts of a bum poem" he'd scrapped, some correspondence with the editor of the *Double Dealer* magazine, and a few journalistic carbons.

"You, naturally, would say, 'Good' etc. But don't say it to me," Ernest went on. "I ain't yet reached that mood. 3 years on the damn stuff, Some like that Paris 1922 I fancied." Hemingway was absolutely right about Pound's reaction to the news. The loss was an "act of Gawd," Pound insisted. "No one is *known* to have lost anything by *suppression* of early work." Besides, memory was "the best critic." All Ernest had lost was the time it would take him to rewrite the parts he could remember. "If the middle, i.e., FORM, of a story is right one ought to be able to reassemble it from memory ... If the thing wobbles and won't reform then it ... never would have been right." All of this was cold comfort. "I thank you for your advice to a young man on the occasion of the loss by stealing of his complete works," Ernest replied with sarcasm. "It is very sound. I thank you again."

We don't know exactly what constituted Hemingway's "complete works" as of December 1922. The available evidence suggests it may not have been as great a loss as it seemed at the time, and it hardly represented three years' work. It was true that Hemingway had been writing stories and sketches since the fall of 1918—13 in all, according to Paul Smith, an authority on Hemingway texts. Ernest sent most of his earliest writing attempts—showy overwritten tales about Italian gangsters, French mercenaries, and the exotic underworld of Wabash Avenue in Chicago—to the *Saturday Evening Post*. "The Saturday Evening Post did not buy them nor did any other magazine," Hemingway observed in retrospect, "and I doubt if worse stories were ever written." He didn't take that material with him, when he and Hadley left for Paris in December 1921; it remained in the attic of the Oak Park home where he had grown up.

Smith believed that Hemingway packed for Europe the beginning of a novel, a sheaf of poems, possibly some war stories set in Italy, and an early draft of "Up in Michigan," a story about a brutal sex encounter that Gertrude Stein declared "inaccrochable"—unfit for public display. That story survived the theft at the Gare de Lyon because Ernest kept it in a separate drawer from the rest of his work. So did "My Old Man," which was in the mail to editors, as well as six poems that had gone to Harriet Monroe at *Poetry*, with Pound's endorsement.

The contents of the valise, then, included Hemingway's novel in progress about a young man named Nick Adams and his experiences in northern Michigan—the novel Stein told him to rewrite, one that Hadley recalled as "a knockout"—and whatever else in the way of stories and poems he managed to produce during a busy 12 months (not three years) in Europe. Over that period, much of his time was taken up by assignments from the *Toronto Star* and skiing, hiking, and fishing trips. He'd logged 10,000 railroad miles during that year.

The "Paris 1922" vignettes that he'd mentioned to Pound were gone, too, but Ernest was able to recover them from memory. These were six "true sentences," five-finger exercises in prose like the imagism Pound had been advocating for poetry. Each of them began "I have watched" or "I have seen" and went on to describe a riveting scene. Some of these Hemingway had really witnessed, some he had not. An example:

> *I have seen Peggy Joyce at 2 a.m. in a dancing in the Rue Caumartin quarreling with the shellacked haired young Chilean who had long pointed finger nails, danced like Rudolph Valentino and shot himself at 3:30 that same morning.*

Ernest had not been at the "dancing." The heiress Peggy Joyce and her Chilean lover danced until 4 a.m., and he shot himself two hours later. The facts were rearranged, but they created an indelible image in the reader's mind.

In letters written in the 1950s, Ernest expanded the inventory of what had been lost to include "good stories about Kansas City" and two "short stories set on the Italian front," while the novel he had "begun" transformed into the novel he had "written." Exaggeration ruled, too, in his fictional recreation of the incident in "The Strange Country." That story, which appears as the last in Hemingway's *Complete Stories*, was written as part of an uncompleted novel he was working on during 1946-47 and 1950-51. The writer-protagonist, Roger, tells his girlfriend the painful story of how his first wife, who was "very beautiful and kind," had lost his work at the Gare de Lyon and how he went to Paris to see for himself:

I remember walking up the stairs and opening the door of the flat, unlocking it and pulling back on the brass handle of the sliding lock and the odor of Eau de Tavel in the kitchen and the dust that had sifted through the windows on the table in the dining room and going to the cupboard where I kept the stuff in the dining room and it was all gone.

When the character saw that there really were "no folders with originals, nor folders with typed copies, nor folders with carbons," he lay down on the bed with a pillow between his legs and his arms around another pillow. His forehead "lay against the Persian shawl that covered the bed which was only a mattress and springs set on the floor and the bed cover was dusty too and [he] smelt the dust and lay there with [his] despair and the pillows were [his] only comfort."

"Eleven stories, a novel, and poems" were gone, the protagonist remembered, and after the discovery, he had a drink with the concierge at his flat, who had seen "monsieur" working at his desk and at the café on the corner "for three years." The concierge was understanding and supportive, which made Roger feel somewhat better. He realized that he might write a better novel, but he missed the lost stories "as though they were a combination of my house, and my job, my only gun, my small savings and my wife." As in the sketch about Peggy Joyce and her lover, concrete detail gives this account greater authenticity.

Three years' lost work became four in a fragment Hemingway cut from *A Moveable Feast*. He and Hadley "had been armoured together by two things," Ernest wrote. "The first was the loss of everything I had written over a period of four years except for two stories and a few poems." It's an odd phrase, "armoured together," suggesting that they could only avoid further emotional wounds by donning protective covering.

The second thing that bonded them, presumably, was Hadley's pregnancy. When she came from Paris to Lausanne she left her precautionary birth control apparatus behind. This was done "not exactly on purpose," she told biographer Alice Sokoloff, although she did think "it would be wonderful to have a baby." Ernest was "so cross" when she told him about it, and not at all pleased when it became clear a few months later that a baby was on its way. He was "too young to be a father," he told Gertrude Stein.

HAREMS AND TRIANGLES

Very likely the Hemingways were in Chamby-sur-Montreux when John Hadley Nicanor Hemingway was conceived. Their stay, from December 1922 through February 1923, was their third at the Gangwisches' chalet. Ernest sang the praises of the place in a letter to Isabelle Simmons of Oak Park, who was going to join them in the mountains. "We'll have a wonderful time," he assured her. They'd go bobsledding and skiing, and do a lot of reading. Chamby and nearby Les Avants constituted "the finest place in the world."

Hadley also rhapsodized about the retreat in a letter to Ernest's mother Grace. On December 11, she and Ernest took a scouting trip from Lausanne to Chamby. They put on their "adored outing togs," took two long runs on their favorite bobsled, had tea with the Gangwisches, and then rushed to catch the train up to Les Avants for a last run, swooping down the snow-covered mountains toward Lake Geneva under a "glorious rosy sunset."

A week later, Ernest and Hadley returned to Chamby from Lausanne and settled in to welcome the others they'd persuaded to visit. The group included Chink and Isabelle, as well as a contingent from St. Louis: the lovely Janet Phelan as well as Dave and Barbara O'Neil, a somewhat older couple who brought sons George and Horton and daughter Barbara along. The O'Neils took rooms at the Grand Hotel in Les Avants for its amenities, "the good food and people and music." Everyone else stayed at the Gangwisches' modest pension.

The winter sports, bracing air, and good company did wonders to relieve Ernest's distress about the lost manuscripts. Years later, Chink remembered how cheerful his friend seemed that Christmas. They went to Les Avants for Christmas dinner, after which "Hem agreed to perform" in an amateur hour. He sang a bawdy song "in some sort of German about a particularly unfortunate family with unlimited domestic troubles." This was "ill-received" by the proper Anglo-American guests; when only Chink and Hadley applauded, Ernest reappeared before the curtain to say, "I seem to have displeased the more respectable members of the audience." Thereafter, Chink recalled, they patronized less stodgy venues.

The group also enjoyed success on the slopes. The four-man bobsled team of Chink, Ernest, and the O'Neil boys won the holiday race on the Col de Sonloup. Hadley and the two Barbaras O'Neil came in second in the women's event. Dorman-Smith returned to his post early in January and was replaced in the group by Isabelle Simmons. Pretty and intelligent, Isabelle grew up down the block from Ernest in Oak Park, but she was a few years younger and they only became friends after he returned from the war. She and Hadley immediately bonded in Chamby. They knitted sweaters and read the same books together, and formed a three-way triad with Ernest—one that would later be replicated with disastrous consequences.

Actually, in Chamby, it was a harem rather than a triad, but one that was innocent enough. The day Izzy arrived, the Paris edition of the *Chicago Tribune* reported from Constantinople that "there was joy in the Sultan's abandoned harem." It was payday, which meant the 11 sultanas had drawn their monthly checks from the nationalist government ranging from 65 to 90 dollars. The following day, Izzy, Hadley, young Barbara O'Neil, and Janet Phelan started calling themselves Hemingway's harem. It was all in good fun; Hadley was happy to share her man in such an amusing way, and Ernest enjoyed the female attention. Three years later, when Isabelle wrote him that she was marrying the scholar Francis R.B. Godolphin, Ernest congratulated her and declared that her place in the harem was "still open and being held open and will be held open and just let ... anybody try to usurp it."

It was probably in Chamby that Hadley and Ernest arrived at a private understanding to cut their hair to the same length and thereby signal their goal to become "the same one." Ernest wrote about it in a piece called "Secret Pleasures," unprinted in the original publication of A Moveable Feast but included in the 2009 restored edition of that book. Hair fetishes—in particular ones in which a man and a woman grow or cut their hair to resemble each other—figure prominently in Hemingway's writing, as in A Farewell to Arms (1929) and The Garden of Eden (published posthumously in 1986).

"Secret Pleasures" suggests that this idea first took root in the winter of 1923, and that it gave both Ernest and Hadley a sexual charge; their conversation in the piece tries to convey this, but it's not quite successful. It all starts when Ernest decides to let his hair grow. Calling her husband "Tatie," one of her pet names for him, Hadley coyly announces,

"Tatie, I thought of something exciting."
"Tell me."
"I don't know whether to say it."
"Say it. Go on. Please say it."
"I thought maybe it could be the same as mine."
"But yours keeps on growing too."
"No. I'll get it just evened tomorrow and then I'll wait for you.
Wouldn't that be fine for us?"
"Yes."

She then says "something secret" and he says "something secret back." It might take four months to even the hair lengths, and other people—"poor unfortunate other people," she says—will think they're crazy. But never mind. "We'll just do it and not worry and have a lovely time." It will be "another secret" they share.

So they played their erotic games together, while unspoken between them lay the terrible hurt of his lost work, the baby she wanted and he didn't, and, quite possibly, the ghost of Agnes von Kurowsky.

In late January, Ernest went to Paris alone, looking for what was not to be found in their flat and—who knows?—lying down afterward with two pillows to comfort the pain. He also made the trip to gather some fresh clothes and books and collect his mail, including the disappointing letter from Agnes that must have arrived by then.

Back in the mountains, snow turned to slush as February wore on, and the Hemingways' winter companions all left. There were only the two of them in Chamby, or rather two plus the child they now knew was on its way. Hadley thought a warm climate would be good for her pregnancy. Ernest was looking for a fresh venue to escape the writer's block that emerged with the loss of his manuscripts. Ezra Pound urged them to come to Rapallo, Italy, where he and Dorothy were wintering. The climate was fine, Pound said. Mike Strater was in town eager for some vigorous exercise, and they could get by at a pension for only 500 lire ($25) a week. Duly encouraged, Ernest and Hadley packed up and took the train to Rapallo.

Hadley's first sight of the Ligurian coast, lush and green even in midwinter, entranced her. She and Ernest kissed as their train went through a tunnel past Genoa. Coming out, she could see olive trees on one side, and on the other the pastel roofs of Rapallo and the very blue sea. "Why didn't you ever tell me about this before?" she asked. Ernest was less impressed with the city, which had been a favorite of writers—Wordsworth and Keats among them—since the late 18th century. "The place ain't much," he wrote Gertrude Stein. The sea looked "weak," it rained a lot, and the Fascist son of their hotel proprietor stared insultingly at the guests.

Sexually he and Hadley were as active as they'd ever been. As Ernest wrote in an unpublished sketch about that time and place, "Cats love in the garden. On the green tea table to be exact. The big cat gets on the small cat. Sweeney gets on Mrs. Porter. Hadley and I ... are happiest in bed. In bed we are well fed. There are no problems in bed."

Out of bed, though, Ernest reverted to his sour mood. The lost valise still rankled, and he had Strater and Pound to indulge him. "You know, Mike," he told Strater, "if you had had those manuscripts in your trunk, you would not have left them to go and get something to read." Pound, more judgmental, "told Robert McAlmon that he thought Hadley had lost the manuscripts deliberately."

Numerous scholars and biographers have explored the potential psychological angles of the incident. In *The Paris Years*, Michael Reynolds suggests that the loss gave Ernest an inescapable advantage in their relationship: "It was different between them now. He saw it in her face. Whatever else happened between them, he would always have this edge. As they hugged and he kissed away her tears, perhaps Hadley knew it as well."

Jeffrey Meyers, writing in his 1985 account, *Hemingway: A Biography*, argues that

> *the loss was irrevocably connected in Hemingway's mind with sexual fidelity ... [He] now had something to hold against her—for he never forgot an injury ... The loss of his creative work when he was in Lausanne probably influenced his fictional portrayal of the loss of Catherine Barkley's baby in Montreux [in A Farewell to Arms]. In the novel he vicariously got rid of the unwanted infant just as Hadley (subconsciously, if not deliberately) got rid of the manuscripts that had kept them apart, day and night.*

In *Hadley*, Diliberto observed that Meyers's comments were "too harsh," like those of others who accused Hadley of "busybodiness," "inexcusable negligence," "silliness," and "stupidity." As an alternative, Diliberto suggests that the loss of the valise may have been caused, at least subconsciously, by Hadley's passive-aggressive personality, and as a parallel, she cites the time Hadley let Ernest's unwelcome Christmas present to her in 1920—a second-hand beaded handbag—slip overboard "accidentally."

Was Hadley's act subversive? Or, as readers of the bestselling *The Paris Wife* keep asking author Paula McClain, was she trying to sabotage his career? Not really, McClain responds, and yet:

Well, of course she was jealous because she felt abandoned. The most important thing in the world to him was his work, and the most important thing in the world to her was him. There is no balance there, and that can be devastating. People also don't like—women don't like—the timing of the loss of the manuscripts and then her becoming pregnant ... It feels slightly manipulative, and yet a woman hearing the pounding of the biological clock, we get it.

It doesn't do to invest too much faith in such speculations. Sometimes a cigar is just a cigar. Whatever motivations may have been at work, there can be no doubt that the lost valise opened a fissure in the Hemingways' marriage. Ernest may not have been writing about it in 1929's *A Farewell to Arms*, but he almost certainly was in *The Garden of Eden*, in which writer David Bourne's wife viciously burns his work in progress.

Despite the rain and the Fascists who dominated

Italian politics at that time, it was in Rapallo that Ernest began to recover from the blow of his missing manuscripts. The agent behind that recovery was a shy American named Edward O'Brien, the compiler of an annual volume of *Best Short Stories* who was staying as a boarder in a monastery above the city. Hemingway showed O'Brien "My Old Man," which had come back, rejected, from *Cosmopolitan*; it was the only thing he had to show. O'Brien was so impressed by the racetrack story, with its echoes of Sherwood Anderson, that he broke his own rules and accepted it for *Best Short Stories* on the spot—even though all the anthologized stories were supposed to have initially appeared in magazines. In fact, he went one step further, dedicating the volume to Hemingway (or "Hemenway," actually, for he got the spelling wrong). That kind of unstinting support gave Ernest the boost he needed to resume writing. He was learning, as his mentor Ryall maintained, that the most important thing in life was not to capitalize on one's gains—any fool could do that—but to profit from one's losses.

When Ernest told O'Brien about his lost work, the editor looked so distressed that Hemingway tried to make *him* feel better. "It was probably good ... to lose early work," he said, "all that stuff you fed the troops." Ernest added that he was going to start writing stories again, and as he said it, "only trying to lie so that [O'Brien] would not feel so bad," he realized it was true. At Cortina d'Ampezzo, his and Hadley's next stop in Italy, where they were united once again with Isabelle Simmons, he wrote "Out of Season"—a story that derives its power from the tension between a fictional husband and wife. In the following few months, he finished polishing the "Paris 1922" vignettes for publication in the *Little Review*, and produced "A Very Short Story," which in its bitter attack on Agnes may have released him from yearning for her.

In September, Ernest and Hadley went to Canada. The impending arrival of their baby was the principal reason for the trip. Both of them felt more secure about medical care across the ocean than in France, and Ernest believed that as a father-to-be he needed the regular salary the *Toronto Star* offered him as a reporter.

He was reluctantly adjusting to the idea of fatherhood. "We're both crazy about having the young feller," he declared in a letter to Bill Horne as he and Hadley were preparing to leave Paris. At the same time, though, he lamented having to take a steady job. "I'm cut out for Romance, rather than business," he told Horne, but romance didn't pay. Ernest was also resentful about the restricted freedom of movement and activity that lay ahead. This is the guiding theme of his short story "Cross-Country Snow," in which George and Nick take a final ski trip together in Switzerland. Nick is married, his wife is pregnant, and they are going to go back to the States, though he doesn't want to. Maybe they will never go skiing again, George says. "We've got to," Nick replies. "It isn't worth while if we can't."

PARTING WAYS WITH THE *STAR*

Hemingway's experience as a regular staffer on the *Toronto Star* could hardly have been worse. He went on the payroll on September 10, and immediately ran afoul of Harry C. Hindmarsh, the assistant managing editor, who was eager to bring the star foreign correspondent down to earth. Ernest was given a series of piddling assignments and no bylines for two weeks. Next, on a venture into investigative reporting, Hemingway produced a highly readable but potentially libelous report that the *Star* chose not to publish. Then, on October 4, when Hadley was nearing her delivery date, Hindmarsh sent Hemingway on the road to cover British Prime Minister Lloyd George's visit to the United States and Canada. Ernest was still on the train from New

York to Toronto when John Hadley Nicanor Hemingway was born early on the morning of October 10. The Hemingways blamed Hindmarsh for sending the expectant father away at such a crucial time, and Ernest resolved to quit the *Star* and return to Paris as soon as possible. He also planned (but never completed) a derogatory story about Hindmarsh, who was married to the daughter of the newspaper's publisher. It was to be called "The Son in Law."

John Hadley, soon to be known as Bumby, turned out to be "a corker of a baby boy," Hadley wrote Isabelle Simmons. Although the birth had not been difficult, she stayed in the hospital for two weeks. One evening Ernest made notes about watching Hadley nurse. "The baby nurses very hard but cannot find the place at first. Then he makes a noise like a little baby pig. He is very small and has a beautiful body. Hadley let me lift up his clothes to look at his legs and back." They were a happy family once Hadley came home. "We get along very well ... Hadley is a good article," Ernest wrote Gertrude Stein at Christmas time. Three weeks later, they sailed back to Paris.

It was a risky venture, for Ernest had cut his ties with the *Star* and they lacked a reliable source of income beyond Hadley's inheritance. During the time in Canada, he'd been too busy and too angry to produce any fiction. As he told Edward O' Brien, he felt "all constipated up with stuff to write." However, once back in Paris and settled in a new apartment at 113 rue Notre Dame des Champs, the stories came almost effortlessly. From February through April of 1924, at the absolute top of his form, Hemingway wrote eight stories that would appear in *In Our Time.* Four of them—"Indian Camp," "The Doctor and the Doctor's Wife," "The End of Something," and "The Three-Day Blow"—were set in northern Michigan. The first two focused on the dysfunctional marriage of Nick Adams's parents, the latter pair on Nick's breakup with Marjorie. Two other stories, "Soldier's Home" and "Mr. and Mrs. Elliot," depicted contrasting attitudes toward love and sex in Europe and America. "Cat in the Rain" and "Cross-Country Snow" addressed the issue of pregnancy.

Ernest wrote either at home, or, when the noise from the sawmill below the apartment reached a crescendo, at the nearby café, La Closerie des Lilas. Hadley saw to it that the duties of fatherhood did not interfere with his work or their play. She was enchanted by Bumby, but quickly rehired Marie Cocotte (Madame Henri Rohrbach) as a housekeeper-cum-nanny whenever the occasion warranted. She and Ernest continued to bond through erotic games. "We lived as savages," he described that period, "and kept our own tribal rules and had our own customs and our own standards, secrets, taboos and delights."

He was also gaining some recognition as a serious writer, both at home and abroad. Edward O'Brien's *Best Short Stories of 1923* came out with its dedication to "Ernest Hemenway." Ford Madox Ford, editor of the *Transatlantic Review,* became an especially ardent admirer. He included "Indian Camp" in the April 1924 issue, placed Hemingway in charge of the magazine for its July and August numbers, and printed "The Doctor and the Doctor's Wife" and "Cross-Country Snow" in the magazine's final two issues in November and December. Edmund Wilson wrote a joint review of his two brief limited-edition books, *in our time* (as it was originally spelled using lowercase letters) and *Three Stories and Ten Poems,* praising them for achieving "more artistic dignity than anything else" written about the war by an American.

This praise was pleasant, but not particularly remunerative. Repeatedly Ernest sent his new stories off to American magazines that paid good money for fiction, and repeatedly they returned them. What he needed was to make his mark with a real book, not a limited edition, and he explored that possibility with a number of literary friends, including O'Brien, Donald Ogden Stewart, and Harold Loeb. By mid-1924, he figured he had nearly enough stories for a full-scale volume with a trade publisher.

SHRINKING ASSETS

Around that time he and Hadley became increasingly worried about the status of her trust funds in St. Louis. Her capital, it turned out, lost about one-third of its value through the mishandling of George Breaker, the St. Louis man Hadley had chosen to look after her investments. Helen Breaker was one of her best friends, and George, her husband, had served as a father figure, giving Hadley away at her wedding.

According to Gioia Diliberto, the unquestioned expert on all matters pertaining to Hadley, the Hemingways instructed Breaker in late 1923 to reinvest $19,000—about one-third of her wealth—that had been tied up in railway bonds. The bonds were losing value, and, as Ernest told Breaker, they were looking for "something ... absolutely safe" as an alternative. What proved to be unsafe was placing their trust in Breaker.

Breaker sold the bonds as instructed. They

brought in less than $11,000, but only $1,089.32 of that amount was deposited in Hadley's bank account. He'd reinvested the rest of the money in other bonds, Breaker maintained, but despite repeated and increasingly frantic communications from Ernest, neither those bonds nor the rest of the cash ever materialized. "Where are the bonds? Or where is the money?" Ernest wrote Breaker. "We are as fond of you as ever but for God's sake come through on this. We've got to know where we stand to be able to order our lives." This appeal elicited empty reassurances, but no action. "The truth was," Diliberto concluded, that "George Breaker had embezzled the money."

Hadley's trust still was worth about $40,000, producing some $2,200 a year in income, enough to support a family of three living economically in Paris. Just as he had with the lost manuscripts, Ernest exaggerated the blow. Now that "we haven't any money," he wrote Pound, "I am going to have to quit writing and I never will have a book published." He thought he might have to take up journalism again to make ends meet.

Despite their shrinking funds, he and Hadley went ahead with a trip to Pamplona, Spain, for the Fiesta of San Fermín for a second successive year—they'd gone there for the bullfights in 1923 and would return in 1925 and 1926. Ernest had been enthusiastically describing the fiesta to his friends, and a sizable contingent joined them in Pamplona in the summer of 1924. Don Stewart was there, and so were Chink Dorman-Smith, George O'Neil, Robert McAlmon, John Dos Passos, his girlfriend Crystal Ross, and Bill and Sally Bird. Stewart remembered it as a kind of male festival, "a glorified college reunion" replete with lots of drinking, street dancing, and—in Stewart's case—a couple of cracked ribs proudly acquired when he and Ernest went into the ring during the morning "amateurs," confronting bulls with padded horns.

The fiesta was "one of the high and memorable times," Stewart thought, even if there were signs of uneasiness in the Hemingways' marriage. Money was becoming a real problem, and Ernest had to borrow 300 francs from McAlmon and 100 francs from Stein to pay their expenses. He also worried that Hadley might be once again pregnant. Ernest kept a record of her periods in a notebook, and according to his calculations, she should have started a period on July 13 ("Cat due," in his domestic parlance). When nothing happened by July 16, he began complaining about it. According to McAlmon, in a later account, after he had broken with Hemingway, Ernest was "most unhappy. He told Hadley it would be no fun anymore if they had too many children at his age. She wouldn't be a good playmate anymore either. He was tragic about it, and Hadley, too, became upset." Finally, Sally Bird intervened on her behalf. "Stop acting like a damn fool and a crybaby," she told Ernest. "You're responsible too. Either you do something about not having it, or you have it."

As it turned out, they did not have to make that choice. The next day, Hadley's period began. "Kitty commenced," Ernest noted.

Back in Paris, Hemingway finished "Big Two-Hearted River," a two-part short story about Nick Adams's solitary fishing trip in northern Michigan. It was the longest story he had yet written and—he knew—one of his very best. It ran to "about 100 pages ... and nothing happens and the country is swell," he wrote Gertrude Stein. He was trying to "do the country like Cézanne," (that is, to write the way Paul Cézanne painted) and sometimes succeeding. "But isn't writing a hard job, though? It used to be easy before I met you."

In a 3,000-word coda that was scrapped before publication, Hemingway expounded on the principles guiding his work. "The only writing that was any good was what you made up, what you imagined," he asserted. Nick Adams in the stories was "never himself [Hemingway]." He hadn't camped out alone on the "Big Two-Hearted River." He hadn't seen an Indian woman having a baby, as in "Indian Camp." He'd made that up, and that "made it good." Ernest was beginning to believe in himself as never before. "He wanted to be a great writer. He was pretty sure he would be."

That newfound confidence seemed justified early in 1925. To put their dwindling finances to best use, the Hemingways sublet their Paris apartment and spent the winter months at Schruns, in the Austrian Vorarlberg, where they could room and board inexpensively, place Bumby in the care of a young Austrian girl, and ski all they wanted. At Schruns, Ernest received two pieces of very good news. The first came from Ernest Walsh, who with Ethel Moorhead was starting a new literary magazine called *This Quarter*. In January 1925, Walsh accepted "Big Two-Hearted River" and sent a check for 1,000 francs in payment—approximately as much as Hemingway had earned from all of his writing during 1924. Meanwhile, Don Stewart and Harold Loeb had been touting Ernest's work to American publishers, and in February both cabled him with the news that Boni & Liveright was going to publish his book of stories, uppercasing the title to *In Our Time*. A telegram and letter from Horace Liveright followed, offering a $200 advance against royalties. DELIGHTED ACCEPT, Hemingway wired back.

Things were definitely looking up for Ernest's career. His fast-paced production of stories had somewhat slowed down, but he knew that publishers in the States were looking for novels, which sold better than volumes of short stories. Perhaps he could write a novel about his expatriate experiences.

He wrote the first draft of that novel, *The Sun Also Rises*, in the late summer of 1925. It revolved around a striking woman Ernest came to know well during that year: Duff Twysden, or in fictional form, Brett Ashley. Born in Yorkshire, England, to ambitious parents, the former Mary Duff Smurthwaite had been presented to the Queen as a debutante, and then gone through two bad marriages, the second one to the English baronet Sir Roger Twysden. They'd had a son together, but, Duff told Ernest, Twysden was an alcoholic who beat her when he was drunk. She'd abandoned husband and son and escaped to Paris with her cousin Pat Guthrie (Mike Campbell in Hemingway's fiction), a likable if ne'er-do-well alcoholic who left a trail of unpaid bills behind him. She and Pat were presumably engaged, but this did not stop Duff from pursuing a number of affairs. She was 32 to Ernest's 26, and a habitué at the bars Hemingway frequented.

Marriage Under Threat

Duff cut her hair short, wore mannish, loose-fitting clothes, and drank too much. She was also unmistakably sexy and though (as Hemingway wrote about Brett, Lady Ashley) she "was not supposed to be beautiful, ... in a room with women who were supposed to be beautiful she killed their looks entirely." Ernest was fascinated by her, and for the first time since Katy Smith threatened their engagement, Hadley became fearful about her marriage. She didn't mind Ernest's attentions to Isabelle Simmons, for she felt sure of his love and had formed a close bond with Isabelle herself.

Duff, however, was different. She was kind to Bumby and friendly to Hadley, but manifestly a man's woman, and one widely experienced in affairs. According to McAlmon's jaundiced account, on the Hemingways' evenings out Ernest flirted with Duff so openly that Hadley would start to cry, and rather than comforting his wife, he would ask someone else to take her home. On other occasions, he saw Duff alone in one watering hole or another. During these solo encounters, she taught him how to have affairs.

Her expertise in this subject appealed to Ernest, who was as eager to learn about adultery from Duff as he had been to absorb political wisdom from the newsman Ryall in Lausanne. In his notebooks, he jotted down some of Duff's teachings: 1) "You must make fantastic statements to cover things," she told him. 2) It was best to have many admirers "so no one will know there is some one you love." And, apparently drawing the line against an affair with Ernest, 3) "We can't do it. You can't hurt people. It's what we believe in in place of God"—a remark Ernest appropriated for *The Sun Also Rises*.

Still, there was chemistry between Ernest and Duff. They were close enough that at least twice when she was "broke to the wide" (in financial distress), she appealed to him for loans. "Please do come at once to Jimmie's bar—real trouble ... SOS. Duff." But the relationship turned sour in the summer of 1925 when Duff—putting her expertise into practice—ran off for a romantic week in St. Jean-de-Luz with Harold Loeb. The handsome Loeb had served as Ernest's benefactor in securing a contract from Boni & Liveright, and during the spring and early summer of 1925, they played a lot of afternoon tennis together. Then Loeb, falling hard for Duff, broke off with his lover Kitty Cannell and arranged the rendezvous in St.-Jean-de Luz. This affair was supposed to be secret, but Ernest knew about it and was deeply jealous. The tension between them erupted at Pamplona.

Once again Ernest collected a group of companions for the annual fiesta. Hadley, a bullfight *aficionado* herself, came along, as did Donald Ogden Stewart. Aside from Loeb, Ernest also recruited Bill Smith who, with Hemingway's encouragement, had come to Paris to seek employment. At the last minute, immediately after her rendezvous with Loeb, Duff decided to join the party as well. "I am coming on the Pamplona trip with Hem and your lot," she wrote in a love letter to Harold. "Can you bear it? With Pat [Guthrie] of course." She'd try to get out of it if Harold insisted, Duff added, but she felt miserable without him. "I'm dying to come and feel that even seeing you and being able to talk to you will be better than nothing." A later letter assured Loeb that "Hem has promised to be good and we ought to have a marvelous time."

They did not. Smith was horrified by the bullfights, and Loeb thought it shameful to watch the agony of the dying bulls. In the evenings Duff's present and potential lovers—Guthrie, Loeb, and Hemingway—exchanged insults and threatened fistfights. The "devil sex" ruined the holiday for Don Stewart, who'd had a wonderful time the previous year. Ernest filed everything away for use in his novel-in-progress, which was centered around the expatriates in Paris and Pamplona. He plunged back into work almost immediately after the trip, transforming Duff into a character for the book. She was no longer a danger to the Hemingway's marriage, so Hadley kept quiet but, unbeknownst to her, a more menacing rival was on the scene.

DOUBLE DUTY

Small in stature, delicate of limb, and fine of feature, the Pfeiffer sisters, Pauline and Virginia (Jinny), wore their bobbed hair in bangs. They were quick of wit, beautifully dressed, and financially well-off. Their father Paul ran a cotton processing plant in Piggott, Arkansas, and had bought 60,000 acres of land in the area. Their generous uncle Gus Pfeiffer, a man of great wealth, owned a substantial interest in Richard Hudnut perfumes. Their mother Mary, a devout Catholic, sent the girls off to boarding school at the Visitation Convent in St. Louis, located close to Hadley's girlhood home. Pauline, the older sister, went on to earn a degree in journalism at the University of Missouri, and worked on newspapers in Cleveland and New York before going abroad to work for the Paris edition of *Vogue*. She was nearly 30, and—some thought—looking for a husband.

Ernest and Hadley met the Pfeiffers in mid-March 1925 at a party given by Harold Loeb and Kitty Cannell (who were back together after Harold's affair with Duff) to celebrate the acceptance of Hemingway's *In Our Time*. Initially, Pauline was not attracted to Ernest, despite his impending success, while he showed more interest in her lesbian sister Jinny. Her second impression, when the Pfeiffers came to visit Ernest and Hadley in their modest apartment, was no more favorable. Pauline liked and felt sorry for Hadley, who in her dowdy clothes did everything around the place while Ernest, lord and master, lay in bed reading, unkempt, unshaven, and uninterested in the women's conversation.

Several visits later, though, and quite to her surprise, Pauline became sexually drawn to Hemingway. She continued to see her "temporary best friend" (as she defined her relationship to Hadley), lavished attention on Bumby, adopted Ernest's enthusiasm for the six-day bike races, and waited for his flare for Duff Twysden to burn out. As Hadley later reflected, Pauline "didn't go straight for my husband. When she made up her mind that he was what she wanted, she was very aggressive ...

She had the guts to spend a lot of violent energy on Ernest. He couldn't help himself."

Hemingway's developing career drew others toward him. It was one thing to journey around the continent reporting on wars and treaties, but quite another to gain acceptance and admiration in literary circles, both among magazine editors and stateside publishers. With his prospects on the rise, he became someone worth knowing. When F. Scott Fitzgerald came to Paris in May, with *The Great Gatsby* just published, he sought out Hemingway. Fitzgerald was tremendously impressed by the up-and-coming novelist, and tried to arrange for Ernest to be published by Scribner's, where the talented and author-friendly Maxwell Perkins could edit both of them. Gerald and Sara Murphy, the attractive and well-off American expatriates, also made a point of looking up Ernest and inviting him to join their circle of artists, musicians, and writers that included Pablo Picasso, Fernand Léger, John Dos Passos, Dorothy Parker, Scott and Zelda Fitzgerald, and Donald Ogden Stewart. Stewart described the Murphys in his autobiography. "Gerald and Sara were both rich. He was handsome; she was beautiful, they had three golden children" and a gift for "making life enchantingly pleasurable for those ... fortunate enough to be their friends."

In her unfashionable clothes, Hadley never felt comfortable with the Murphys, who came from old money and did everything with cultured grace. The stylish Pauline was more their cup of tea.

In the fall of 1925, having completed the first draft of *The Sun Also Rises*, Ernest set that book aside to participate in an act of literary duplicity. In a 10-day period before and after Thanksgiving, he cranked out a parody of his benefactor Sherwood Anderson's *Dark Laughter* (1925) to be called *The Torrents of Spring*. Hadley and Bumby were both suffering from bad colds at the time, and Pauline came by often to visit with Hadley and to praise the latest installment of Ernest's comic fable in progress. He also read parts of this script aloud to others, including Dos Passos and Fitzgerald.

The listeners were divided in their reaction. Hadley and Dos Passos both advised against publishing the book. Sherwood Anderson had been helpful to Hemingway in Chicago, and when he came to Paris, he had written a strong blurb for *In Our Time*. He was a friend and did not deserve such treatment, they argued. Pauline, on the other hand, thought *The Torrents of Spring* brilliantly funny, as did Fitzgerald, who called it in a letter to Horace Liveright "about the best comic book ever written by an American."

At that time, Hemingway, though only 26, was suddenly becoming a hot literary property. *In Our Time* came out in a small printing, but despite minimal advertising from Boni & Liveright, it was earning excellent reviews. Moreover, word was circulating in New York and in Paris about the commercial promise of *The Sun Also Rises*, his novel-in-progress. For several months, Fitzgerald had been urging Perkins to go after Hemingway, and author Louis Bromfield was encouraging his publisher Alfred Harcourt to do the same. Both Scribner's and Harcourt were ready to make generous offers if Hemingway left Liveright.

Retrospectively, it seems clear that Ernest composed his parody of Anderson in order to break with Liveright. The contract specified that the firm would publish two Hemingway books after *In Our Time*, and that one of the two was to be a novel. But it offered Hemingway a way out of this commitment if the publishers rejected a book he submitted.

The Torrents of Spring, Hemingway knew, was almost certain to be such a contract-breaker. Sherwood Anderson was one of Boni & Liveright's best-selling authors, and the publishers would most likely have to turn down a book that "viciously" (Liveright's word) satirized him. Hemingway's parody did double duty, then, offering him a pathway to a more attractive publisher while repudiating those reviewers of In Our Time who declared that his stories were influenced by Anderson.

Ernest's strategy became apparent in his correspondence with Ezra Pound. On November 30, he wrote Pound that Torrents was "probably unprintable, but funny as hell. Wrote it to destroy Sherwood and various others." Hemingway overvalued his short book. Torrents has some engaging moments of verbal slapstick, but Hemingway lacked the gift for lighthearted nonsense (or "crazy humor") of such contemporaries as Stewart and Robert Benchley.

On December 7, he mailed the short, 28,000-word book to Horace Liveright with a letter demanding a $500 advance, a sizable printing, and the kind of promotion Boni & Liveright failed to give In Our Time. It was true that he was making fun of Anderson, he told Liveright, but no one "with any stuff" could be damaged by satire. Besides, the publishers should welcome the chance to differentiate between the two authors. "[Y]ou might as well have us both under the same roof and get it coming and going"—that is, with Hemingway coming and Anderson on his way out. If Liveright decided against publishing the book, Ernest acknowledged, he had a number of other propositions to consider. But, he wrote in closing, "I want you to publish it ... because it is a hell of a fine book and it can make us both a hell of a lot of money." Ernest instructed Liveright to cable him "at once" with his decision. Nowhere in the letter did he mention *The Sun Also Rises*.

Three weeks later, on December 30, the cable from Horace Liveright arrived: "REJECTING TORRENTS OF SPRING. PATIENTLY AWAITING MANUSCRIPT SUN ALSO RISES. WRITING FULLY." According to the promised letter, none of Boni & Liveright's in-house readers liked *Torrents*. The book sketched a bitter caricature of Sherwood Anderson and was virtually unmarketable, Liveright pointed out. "Really, old top," he inquired of Hemingway with a trace of sarcasm, "even admitting that *Torrents of Spring* is a good American satire, who on earth do you think would buy it?"

CHANGING PUBLISHERS

This letter carefully avoided mentioning the terms of the three-book contract, which mandated that if Boni & Liveright did not exercise their option to publish a second book within 60 days of its submission, the firm's option rights to the third book would lapse. Ernest, however, understood these terms very well. On the day after receiving Liveright's cable, and without waiting for the full explanation, Hemingway wrote Fitzgerald a long letter enlisting his aid.

"I have known all along that they could not and would not be able to publish [*Torrents*] as it makes a bum out of their present ace and best seller Anderson," Hemingway admitted. "I did not, however, have that in mind when I wrote it," he disingenuously added, before describing in detail the provisions of his contract with Boni & Liveright. He was therefore "loose," Ernest asserted, "[n]o matter what Horace may think up in his letter to say." Now he was relying on Fitzgerald to pave the way with Maxwell Perkins at Scribner's.

It was important to move rapidly, Ernest told Fitzgerald, for there was competition on the field. He'd been approached by William Aspinwall Bradley from Knopf, and Alfred Harcourt had written Bromfield asking to see the "Anderson piece," and commenting that "Hemingway's first novel might rock the country." Then Ernest outlined his plan: He would wire Liveright to send the typescript of *Torrents* to Don Stewart at the Yale Club in New York City, and Stewart would deliver it to Perkins. Meanwhile, Fitzgerald was to "write Max[well Perkins] telling him how Liveright turned it down and why and your own opinion of it. I am rewriting *The Sun Also Rises*, and it is damned good. It will be ready in 2-3 months for late fall or later if they wish."

He was jeopardizing his chances with Harcourt by approaching Fitzgerald, Ernest added, and was only doing so because of his friendship with Scott and the favorable impression he'd formed of Perkins. In reality, Ernest had good reasons to be inclined in Perkins' favor. In a letter written before (but received after) Hemingway went under contract with Liveright for *In Our Time*, Perkins asked for a chance to see any book-length work of his. Also, the celebrated editor had been instrumental in shaping Fitzgerald's meteoric rise—five books in five years from 1920 to 1925—and he promised to remain "absolutely loyal to authors" he and Scribner's believed in.

Hemingway specifically asked Fitzgerald to mark his letter to Perkins for the mail boats leaving January 5, so it would reach New York as soon as possible. Fitzgerald moved even quicker, cabling Perkins on January 8:

YOU CAN GET HEMINGWAYS FINISHED

NOVEL PROVIDED YOU PUBLISH UNPROMISING SATIRE. HARCOURT HAS MADE DEFINITE OFFER. WIRE IMMEDIATELY WITHOUT QUALIFICATIONS. Perkins cabled back at once: *PUBLISH NOVEL AT FIFTEEN PERCENT AND ADVANCE IF DESIRED. ALSO SATIRE UNLESS OBJECTIONABLE OTHER THAN FINANCIALLY.*

Two days later, fearing that the "qualification" vis-à-vis *Torrents* might be "fatal," Perkins sent Fitzgerald a still more positive cable: CONFIDENCE ABSOLUTE. KEEN TO PUBLISH HIM.

On a trip to New York early in February 1926, Hemingway stopped in at Boni & Liveright to officially cut ties with the publisher (the requisite 60 days had passed). Among other things he assured Horace Liveright that he'd acted "in good faith" throughout, an issue Liveright had not raised. The next day he went to Scribner's and signed a contract for both books on favorable terms, netting an advance of $1,500 against a 15 percent royalty.

"I am extremely grateful to you for intervening about Hemingway," Perkins wrote Fitzgerald. In a letter that crossed Perkins's, Fitzgerald warned the editor—somewhat after the fact—to be sure to *"get a signed contract"* for The Sun Also Rises, for Hemingway was "temperamental in business" matters. That comment was confidential, he added, directing Perkins to "please destroy this letter."

Fitzgerald's observations suggest he was surprised by Hemingway's calculated efforts to get "loose" from Liveright. This seems a bit odd, as there was nothing particularly wrong with changing publishers. Writers did it all the time, and publishers were always on the lookout for promising authors. In June 1925, in fact, Liveright had asked Hemingway to line up other writers for his firm. Ernest responded sarcastically that "grabbing off" writers was beyond his capabilities as a simple country boy from Chicago.

Or maybe everything wasn't so simple. Ernest had become convinced, as of early 1925, that the whole world was "crooked" and that nearly everything depended upon influence. Why *shouldn't* he use Fitzgerald to his advantage in his dealings with Scribner's? Scott was more than eager to help him, for he had formed a strong attachment to Ernest and very much wanted to solidify their friendship and be published alongside him. As proof of his dedication, Fitzgerald persuaded Hemingway to cut two and a half pages from the opening of his story "Fifty

Grand" and then sent it off to Scribner's with his endorsement. One benefit of writing books for Scribner's, he told Ernest, included good access to the monthly magazine the firm also published, which paid fairly well for fiction. That didn't work out in this case, for *Scribner's* magazine thought "Fifty Grand" too long, even after the deleted beginning. (Eventually, the story appeared in the *Atlantic Monthly*.)

"Fifty Grand" is about a prizefighter who agrees to throw a fight for money. Ernest would reprise this theme in "The Killers," his first story to appear in *Scribner's* in 1927. In that story, a double cross leads to the death of the boxer Ole Andreson. An echo of the premise can also be found in "My Old Man," about a jockey paid off to lose a race. Manifestly, Hemingway was interested in the human capacity for double-dealing. It was inadvisable, he liked to say, to bet on any animal that could talk. At that time, surreptitious arrangements of dubious morality, both in his career and his private life, were much on his mind.

The most curious thing about the contract-breaking episode is that Hemingway did not admit to anyone—not to Fitzgerald or Pound, not to Liveright or Perkins, not to Hadley or Pauline, not even to himself—that he accomplished it with an unusual degree of calculation. In effect, he had deliberately interrupted the most serious creative work of his life so far—*The Sun Also Rises*—to produce the 10-day wonder *Torrents of Spring*, which he proceeded to wield as a tool to separate himself from his relationship with Liveright and change publishers to Scribner's. In a "crooked" world, one had to look out for himself.

It is possible, if unlikely, that Hemingway really thought *Torrents* was a wonderful literary work. Pauline assured him that it was absolutely hilarious, and—clearly unaware of what was afoot—she even volunteered to accompany him to New York to assure everyone at Boni & Liveright about its merits. Hadley had said no to the book. Pauline said yes to that, and everything else.

She had ingratiated herself into the Hemingway family as a friend, but would become Ernest's lover. Gioia Diliberto's invaluable digging unearthed a plausible account, in an unpublished Hemingway fragment, of how that happened.

> *[Pauline] was a nice girl and easy to talk to and said funny things and admired him ... very much ... and thought he was a fine writer and as his wife had bronchitis then and coughed a great deal and as [the girl] never coughed at all and seemed impervious to*

colds, even in Paris, and in a little while, without knowing it, through talk and having things in common and she being very attractive and admiring him to start with and he never having gone with any other woman before he was married now five years and she being such a nice girl at the corner of course he was in love with her.

One night there was no cab and he walked with her along the rue d'Assas looking for one, or rather walking and forgetting to look for one and them both excited by each other and dinner waiting at home. He put his arm around her and kissed her and she kissed him there on the sidewalk in the dark and he told her that he loved her. A cab came along and he put her in it and said, "Good night, darling."

She said, "Good night, my dear," and he went home to his dinner sick inside with excitement and was especially nice to his wife whom he loved very dearly and felt full of remorse for and they had a very loving time and she never suspected anything and was pleased he loved her so.

Once the affair began, Pauline became more aggressive about being an integral part of the Hemingways' life. Pauline "is a swell girl," Ernest wrote Bill Smith on December 3, 1925. "Her and

Hash [his nickname for Hadley] and I are together all the time. She and I have done some A1 drinking." On a Sunday around that time—probably November 29, and possibly to celebrate finishing *Torrents*—he and Pauline killed "two bottles of Beaune, a bottle of Chambertin and a bottle of Pommard and with the aid of Dos Passos a [quart] of Haig in the square bottle, and a quart of hot Kirsch." Once Hadley had been his heroic female drinking companion. Now Pauline assumed that role.

Not only that, but she arranged to spend 10 days over Christmas with Ernest, Hadley, and Bumby in Schruns. Pauline did very little skiing, staying in her room reading while Ernest and Hadley ventured on the slopes. But she was there for dinner, and the three-handed bridge game afterward that Hadley invariably lost, and in a room down the hall. Ernest began certifying their status as a triangle, dubbing himself Drum, Hadley Dulla, and Pauline Doubladulla. Hadley was distressed by the intimations of disloyalty in this private language, but did not object. Her tendency was to back away from confrontations. Perhaps, she thought, if she kept silent the crisis might blow over.

THE END AND AFTER

Hadley considered accompanying Ernest on his trip to New York to straighten out his book publishing entanglements, but was reluctant to put an ocean between herself and Bumby and decided to stay at Schruns. So her husband was on his own, first for a week in Paris, and then for nearly three weeks abroad. Pauline saw as much of Ernest as she could in Paris, even though her workload at *Vogue* was heavy, with spring fashion previews coming up. She sent reports of these meetings to Hadley, maintaining her status as best friend. On January 29, she wrote, "I've seen your husband E. Hemingway several times—sandwiched in like good red meat between thick slices of soggy bread." On February 4, the day after Ernest sailed, she wrote Hadley again. "Your husband, Ernest, was a delight to me. I tried to see him as much as he would see me and was possible."

Hadley was hardly reassured by "your husband" comments. Or by Pauline's promises in the second letter to send Hadley a blue kimono and to include Bumby in her will, now that she was well set up with a sizable trust fund of her own. She felt lonely without Ernest and apprehensive about his activities on the road. Hadley was briefly heartened when

Ernest wrote her about the $1,500 advance and 15 percent royalty contract with Scribner's. "Quite a boy, Hemingway. I feel pretty proud," she wrote Isabelle Simmons Godolphin, adding that they were planning to come to the United States in the fall. Her mood darkened with word that Ernest's ship, the *President Roosevelt*, had encountered bad weather in the North Atlantic and would arrive several days late. Even worse, her husband would "surely have to stop in Paris for money and to do something about their sublet apartment." That meant he'd be seeing Pauline again. "Please excuse me if I wail," she wrote Isabelle, a graduate from the harem who had become her real and abiding friend.

Pauline and Hadley were both attractive, but about as different as two women could be. Pauline was bright and clever, well-read and stylish, not really pretty but small and slim and nicely put together, devoutly Catholic. And she was desperately in love with Ernest whom she wanted to marry, as determined as a terrier in pursuit of that goal. In contrast, Hadley was thoughtful and quiet, tall and perhaps slightly overweight, beautiful in repose, not at all religious, passive and retiring. But she had one thing in common with Pauline: she too was desperately in love with Ernest, a husband who was slipping away from her.

THE DUPLICITY

Ernest came back to Paris, and Pauline was there to greet him. This is how he remembered their meeting in one of the passages deleted from *A Moveable Feast*:

> *I should have caught the first train [to Schruns] from the Gare de l'Est. But the girl I was in love with was in Paris then ... and where we went and what we did, and the unbelievable wrenching, killing happiness, selfishness and treachery of everything we did gave me such a terrible remorse [that] I did not take the first train or the second or the third.*

When he finally reached Schruns, he spotted Hadley "standing by the tracks." Pulling into the station, he wrote,

> *I wished I had died before I ever loved anyone but her. She was smiling, the sun on her lovely face tanned by the snow and sun, beautifully built, her hair red gold in the sun, grown out all winter awkwardly and beautifully, and Mr. Bumby standing with her blonde and chunky and with winter cheeks looking like a good Vorarlberg boy.*

For a while thereafter, he and Hadley had "a lovely magic time" together. Gerald and Sara Murphy, along with John Dos Passos, came to visit in March, and Ernest tried to teach them how to ski. Gerald, who was 12 years older, started calling Ernest "Papa" for his instructive attitude. The nickname stayed with Hemingway for the rest of his life, and appropriately so, for as an autodidact he was eager to learn how to do things and to convey his knowledge to others. The Murphys, charming as ever, persuaded Ernest to read a few chapters of *The Sun Also Rises* aloud and praised it so fervently that he—a trusting and foolish bird dog in their presence—virtually "wagged his tail with pleasure." Then the visitors were gone, but not before inviting the Hemingways to visit them at Villa America, their place in Antibes, France, in May. As spring came to the mountains, Ernest spent every morning revising his novel, and he and Hadley "loved and trusted each other truly." It seemed to him that they were "invulnerable again" and he would not "get back into the badness" of infidelity.

Every day, though, brought a letter from Pauline. And as soon as they got back to Paris, she and her sister Jinny whisked Hadley off on a trip to the Loire Valley—probably, it seems, to let Hadley know about her husband's relationship with Pauline. No confessions were made, but Pauline was so unusually abrupt, even rude, that Hadley finally asked Jinny if her bad temper had anything to do with Ernest. "I think," Jinny said, choosing her words carefully, "they are very fond of each other."

That gave Hadley something to worry about. As the Paris spring wore on, dark and wet outside, she once more developed a chest cold, Bumby seemed to be coming down with whooping cough, and Ernest had trouble sleeping. He resumed his affair with Pauline, and attempted, in an unpublished sketch, to justify it as

> *a good thing ... or at least not a bad thing. He got something from [Pauline] that he did not get from his wife ... He liked the excitement of the mistress ... and it made him treat [Hadley] better ... [I]t was all right as long as [Hadley] did not know. [Pauline] ... thought it a great sin, however, and it was only justified to her by how much they loved each other. Even then it was not justified.*

Certainly Pauline was not content to just be Ernest's mistress. In an outtake from *A Moveable Feast*, written many years after the affair, he reimagined how she must have felt:

The new one is not happy then because she can see that you love them both although she is still settling for that. When you are alone with her she knows you love her and she believes that if someone loves someone they cannot love anyone else and you never speak about the other to help her and to help yourself although you are past help. You never know and maybe she did not know when she made her decision but sometime in the middle of winter she began to move steadily and relentlessly toward marriage; never breaking her friendship with your wife, never losing any advantage of position...

The new and strange girl that now owned half of you, once she had decided to marry, you could not say decided to break up the marriage because that was only a necessary step, a regrettable step ... made only one mistake. She undervalued the power of remorse.

With their marriage anything but "invulnerable," and not wanting to make trouble but overcome by her doubts nevertheless, Hadley confronted Ernest. Was he in love with Pauline? Were they sleeping together? In response, he chided her for bringing the issue up. Then he stomped out to walk the streets in the rain, leaving Hadley desolate.

With Bumby still ailing, Hemingway decamped

for the bullfights in Madrid early in May. A few days later, Hadley took Bumby to Cap d'Antibes to stay in the Murphys' guesthouse while awaiting Ernest's arrival from Spain. The child was still coughing, though, and the Murphys, fearful for their own three children's health, had him examined by their doctor. The diagnosis was whooping cough, so Hadley and Bumby were quarantined some distance away, at a villa in Juan-les-Pins that the Fitzgeralds rented and then abandoned for a larger one. Hadley summoned Madame Rohrbach to help during the quarantine, and resigned herself to missing not only Ernest, but also much of the lively social life at the Villa America.

Archie and Ada MacLeish were another addition to the Murphys' circle of friends on the Riviera. The MacLeishes had come to Paris in the fall of 1923 after Archie gave up a promising career at a Boston law firm to reinvent himself as a poet. Ada, with her silver voice, studied with the famous composer and teacher Nadia Boulanger.

After three weeks in Spain, Ernest arrived on the scene and was immediately fêted by the Murphys at a champagne-and-caviar party. At the event, Scott Fitzgerald indulged in drunken misbehavior, making derogatory remarks about how pretentious it was to have caviar and champagne, staring rudely at a pretty girl at a nearby table, and lobbing ashtrays toward other guests.

The following day, Fitzgerald was extremely contrite and apologetic—his usual manner after such outbursts. Again, he proved himself a good friend to Hemingway by reading and offering editorial advice about *The Sun Also Rises*, which by this time Ernest had sent to Max Perkins as ready for publication. As with Hemingway's short story "Fifty Grand," Scott recommended cuts in the opening sections of the novel. The first chapter began in a chatty, rather flippant tone.

> *This is a novel about a lady. Her name is Lady Ashley and when the story begins she is living in Paris and it is Spring. That should be a good setting for a romantic and highly moral story. As everyone knows, Spring in Paris is a very happy and romantic time. Autumn in Paris, although very beautiful, might give a note of sadness or melancholy that we shall try to keep out of the story.*

This was followed by biographical information about Brett and her two previous marriages, and her alliance with Mike Campbell, his bankruptcy, and their drinking habits.

In the second chapter, Jake Barnes (the main

character) self-consciously introduces himself as narrator.

So my name is Jacob Barnes and I am writing this story, not as I believe is usual in these cases, from a desire for confession, because being a Roman Catholic I am spared that Protestant urge to literary production, nor to set things all out the way they happened for the good of some future generation, nor any other of the usual highly moral urges, but because I believe it is a good story.

Jake went on from there to describe his job with the Continental Press Association and to deliver a number of cynical comments on Montparnasse and its inhabitants. These included Robert Cohn, "one of the non-Nordic heroes of this book," and Cohn's friend Braddocks (Ford Madox Ford), who Jake would have left out of the story except that he was a friend of Cohn's, and "Cohn is the hero."

In his carefully written critique, Fitzgerald came down hard on this beginning. It gave an impression of "condescending *casualness*" and "elephantine facetiousness." Jake's wise-guy comments on the Latin Quarter were full of "sneers, superiorities and nose-thumbings-at-nothing" that wouldn't do at all. Neither would the background information on Brett and Mike. "That biography from you," he reminded Ernest, "who always believed in the superiority (the preferability) of the *imagined* to the *seen not to say to the merely recounted*." Instead of *showing* what happened in scene and picture, Hemingway was lazily *telling* the story. And it didn't matter that Brett's history was factually drawn from her real-life model, Duff Twysden.

The rest of the book was first-rate, Scott said, but he recommended scrapping the start. Ernest saw his wisdom, cut about 4,000 words, and sent the revised version to Perkins as more or less his own idea. It was a good thing for Hemingway's reputation—and for readers ever after—that Fitzgerald put his mind to work on *The Sun Also Rises*.

In due course, Pauline Pfeiffer, who'd had whooping cough as a child, came to the Riviera to share the Hemingways' holiday. She and Ernest and Hadley rented two rooms at a hotel in Juan-les-Pins, establishing a *ménage à trois* of sorts while Bumby and Madame Rohrbach occupied a small bungalow nearby. The three of them sunned and swam on the beach in the morning, had lunch, took siestas, went on afternoon bicycle rides and gathered for cocktails in the evening with the Murphys, MacLeishes, and Fitzgeralds. The three did almost everything together, except for siesta time and some nights when Ernest left Hadley in their room to join Pauline down the hall. Hadley felt powerless to stop what was happening.

Early in July, the Hemingways took Pauline and the Murphys to Pamplona for yet another, if very different, fiesta. Gerald paid for the best seats at the bullfights, and like Don Stewart two years earlier, accompanied Ernest into the ring for the morning amateurs. He used his raincoat to divert the charging animals, but did so rather awkwardly. "Next year I'll do better, Papa," he said. But there would be no next year for the Murphys at Pamplona, and no next year for Ernest and Hadley as husband and wife.

At the fiesta, Hadley must have felt outnumbered, not only by Pauline but also by the Murphys, who'd decided it would be a good thing for Ernest to change wives. They both liked Pauline, and Sara Murphy, especially, felt that Hadley was too passive and had not kept up with her husband's rapidly ascending career.

Ernest and Hadley went on to Madrid and Valencia after the fiesta, while Pauline returned to Paris and the Murphys to Villa America. But what had been done—in Paris, perhaps in Schruns, and surely at Juan-les-Pins—could not be undone. On May 23, 1926, Ernest wrote his father that he, Hadley and Bumby were planning on coming back to the

U.S. in the fall and then spending the winter in a house in Piggott with Pauline Pfeiffer. By July 24, though, those plans were abandoned.

"Everything is all shot to hell in every direction," Ernest wrote Mike Strater, without saying why. He was similarly vague in a letter to Sherwood Anderson. Every fall, Ernest said, he became homesick for America, but now "Piggott [was] shot to hell along with a lot of other things."

What went unmentioned in this correspondence was that when Ernest and Hadley took the train back to Paris in August, it was to establish separate residences. To make the transition easier, Gerald Murphy offered to let Ernest live in his studio temporarily and deposited $400 in his depleted bank account. In a later letter, Gerald encouraged Ernest to break "cleanly and sharply," for Hadley's "slower tempo" would only hold him back. "Bless you & don't ever budge," he advised.

THE DESPAIR OF TWO WOMEN

But Hadley's show of love for Ernest and her kindness during the separation made it difficult for him to comply with Murphy's suggestion and break off the marriage "cleanly and sharply." As always, she saw matters from his point of view, and no matter what he'd done and was doing, she did not stop loving him. She volunteered to come to his studio and do housekeeping, signing herself "Your loving mummy." She also set aside her own despair to sympathize with his feelings of guilt and remorse. "Ernest felt very sorry that he was doing this to me," she told biographer Alice Sokoloff. "It made me suffer to see the way he suffered ... I don't think he ever did get over it, but I tried to make him feel it was all right."

In mid-September, Hadley stipulated that if Ernest and Pauline agreed to stay apart for a hundred days and still wanted to be married, she would not contest a divorce. The only way they could stick to that provision, the lovers felt, was to put an ocean between them. Pauline sailed from Cherbourg, France, on September 24, spent a few days in New York socializing with friends, and proceeded to her parents' home in Piggott.

Initially, Pauline welcomed the hundred-day provision, thinking of it as a period of suffering for her sins. But back home in Arkansas, alone with her thoughts, the suffering descended into a "madhouse" depression. "I don't know what caused it," she wrote Ernest, "except perhaps God." In the throes of despondency, perhaps after talking matters over with her devoutly Catholic mother or a priest, and reaching rather desperately for atonement, Pauline wrote Hadley offering to extend the hundred-day arrangement. Hadley's promise to permit a divorce after the original period "was a very swell thing to do," she said. But she thought Hadley might regret the promise, might think Pauline and Ernest didn't really love each other, might fear that "something permanent [was] being ended for something passing." And if so, Hadley could take back the promise "and act only when you are so inclined. I know I love Ernest and always will, but you may not be sure of this, and it's things people do when they aren't sure that they regret." In a nobility contest, Pauline was on shaky ground vis-à-vis Hadley, yet her offer was undoubtedly genuine.

Reading about Pauline's severe melancholy, Ernest plunged into a depression of his own. In nightmares, he imagined Pauline deciding that her nerves were shot and she would not go through with the plan. He wrote her that he was contemplating suicide (and not for the first or last time). If he were gone, Pauline's sin would be wiped away, and Hadley would not have to go through with the divorce. But, he added, he would not kill himself until she came back to Paris. Together they might be able to fight off the worst of it.

Meanwhile, the days passed slowly. Ernest

managed to get some work done at Murphy's studio, reading proof on *The Sun Also Rises*, but he was miserably lonely and inevitably turned to Hadley for relief—and, very likely, sex. In an unpublished sketch of his from that time, a separated husband and wife make love, and afterward, somewhat cynically, he thanks her "very much for the very pleasant time." She slaps his face hard, twice. "Go away," she tells him. "Go on away," and begins to cry. For a few moments, in bed together, she'd thought that "everything was all right."

The next day, the husband wakes up "sick inside himself." He had broken up both his life and his wife's because "he and this girl had something which justified anything they did ... Everything had been sacrificed to whatever it was that they had and now he had been unfaithful to that and she was not there so that he could wipe it out with her."

Whether they had sex or not, Ernest got in the habit of stopping by to see Hadley almost every day at the hotel she was staying in, across from the Closerie des Lilas. They had practical matters to discuss involving money, the apartment (still being sublet), and Bumby. Sometimes these discussions ended in quarrels. Ernest even tried to enlist Hadley's sympathy for Pauline's distress; she "was just ripping herself apart," he told his wife. But as the injured party, Hadley could not bring herself to think kindly of the woman who was breaking up her marriage.

On October 16, she called an end to any further wrenching encounters with Ernest. "Dearest Tatie," she wrote him, suggesting "it would be the very best thing" for them to keep apart and felt sure he would agree. When they were lonely, they must "see other people or something." She reminded him that if anything were to happen to her ("not trying to suggest disasters"), he'd be "responsible for Umpster [Bumby]." But she wouldn't be going along on the bicycle trip he'd been planning, or anywhere else, she explained in the letter.

> *Anyway, here's my awfully tender, sorry love, dear Chickie and I don't think Pauline is a rotter and I'm sure some day—if let alone—my old trusting affection for her will come back ... I promise to try for it. But ... I can't afford to think about you two for a while, or I'm going to break down completely. Your loving, oh so sorry we talked again, Cat.*

Still, Ernest had certain husbandly obligations. When Hadley moved from the hotel to an apartment of her own, she sent him a list of things to be delivered there from the Notre Dame les Champs

122

flat, including furniture. He did the work himself, and gladly.

As word of the breakup circulated Paris, Ernest's friends asked him what had happened. Their life had gone to hell, he told Fitzgerald, and it was his fault alone, his entirely—Hadley had been as wonderful as ever. Why did it happen? Bill Bird asked. "Because I am a son of a bitch," Ernest answered. He may have hoped that disparaging himself to others offered a form of absolution.

In a similar vein, Ernest seemed intent on doing whatever he could for the wife he was leaving behind. In late August, as they were about to separate, he sent Perkins the dedication for *The Sun Also Rises*: THIS BOOK IS FOR HADLEY AND FOR JOHN NICANOR HADLEY. Late in November, he instructed Scribner's and Jonathan Cape (his English publisher) to send all royalties from the novel to Hadley. Having hurt her so terribly, he wrote her; it was the least he could do. Without her "loyal and self-sacrificing and always stimulating and loving—and actual cash support," he'd never have been able to write the stories and the novel. As for funds, he could always borrow from wealthy friends or rely on contributions from Pauline's Uncle Gus. "I pray God always that he will make up to you the very great hurt that I have done you—who are the best and truest and loveliest person that I have ever known."

Responding the next evening, Hadley accepted the royalties with thanks, called off the hundred-days agreement, and told Ernest the divorce could go ahead. She asked him to collect his suitcases, and counseled him with her "Mummy's love" to take good care of himself and work well. That was the end. The marriage was over.

All of the Hemingways' friends knew about their breakup, but Ernest withheld the news from his parents in Oak Park. He knew they would disapprove and would do so as vigorously as, say, his mother had condemned *The Sun Also Rises* in her letter to him on December 4, 1926. "Surely you have other words in your vocabulary besides 'damn' and 'bitch,'" she complained. "Every page fills me with a sick loathing." Now *that* was a bad review.

Even after Pauline returned from her three months in exile, Ernest kept silent—or nearly so—about his divorce and impending new marriage. Early in February 1927, he confessed to his parents that he and Hadley had separated but remained the best of friends, and added the dubious claim that he was leading a "monastic life." Rather humiliatingly, Clarence and Grace Hemingway got the news about their son's divorce from the Detroit, Boyne City, and

Chicago newspapers. And they were still unaware of his May 10 marriage to Pauline when, in early August, his father sent Ernest the letter he must have been dreading.

"Oh Ernest," his father wrote. How could he have left Hadley and Bumby? "Your dear mother and I have been heart broken over your conduct." The family "had never had such an incident before." At any rate, he hoped Ernest might still make [his] getaway from that individual who split [his] home."

Answering a month later, Ernest appealed for sympathy and explained what had happened, albeit in a way that stretched the truth. His father's letter consigned "all the 'Love Pirates'"—people who break up homes—to hell. But, Ernest replied, he himself had "seen, suffered, and been through enough" during his "year of tragedy" not to "wish any one in hell." He hadn't written, he said, because he couldn't bring himself to talk about such painful matters. It was because of his desire to keep his private life to himself and not to become a public performer that he had caused his parents so much anxiety.

Meanwhile, he assured his parents, he had done nothing to cause them shame. He loved Hadley, and he loved Bumby. He and Hadley had split up, but he had not deserted her nor was he committing adultery with anyone. The trouble between them had been going on for a long time, and eventually she "decided she wanted the definite divorce." There was no scandal and no disgrace. The breakup was entirely his fault because, for over a year, he had been in love with two women at the same time. But, he added, he had been "absolutely faithful to Hadley" during that period.

He would never stop loving Hadley and Bumby—he hadn't lost Bumby, nor would he—and would continue to look after them. He would also "never stop loving Pauline Pfeiffer to whom I am married," he wrote, mentioning his new wife's name and their marriage for the first time at the bottom of the second typewritten page. He now had responsibility for three people instead of one. He had done nothing to feel ashamed of, either in his life or his work.

His father accepted all of Ernest's assertions. "I am so pleased to hear from you," he replied on September 28. "No more mention of this matter."

THE END — AND NEW BEGINNINGS

Ernest and Pauline had two sons, Patrick and Gregory. They moved to Key West, into a house largely financed by Gus Pfeiffer, who saw to it that money was not an issue. They went to Bimini, in the Bahamas, for deep-sea fishing, and on safari to Africa to hunt big game. While married to Pauline, Ernest may have had an affair with the beautiful Jane Mason that did not last. In the summer of 1936, he published "The Snows of Kilimanjaro." The writer-protagonist of that long story condemns himself for letting his talent dwindle away in a marriage to a rich wife. "It was strange, too, wasn't it," he reflects, "that when he fell in love with another woman, that woman should always have more money than the last one?"

In December 1936, blonde and long-legged Martha Gellhorn, a talented young writer and journalist with roots in St. Louis, stopped into Sloppy Joe's in Key West, where Hemingway did much of his drinking. She and Ernest met and liked each other, and in due course—during and after their shared experience covering the Spanish Civil War—they became lovers and eventually married. The end with Pauline was patterned after the breakup with Hadley—Ernest's adultery and a next wife waiting in the wings. A kind of ironic justice was in operation: serial affairs, serial wives.

In 1933, Hadley married Paul Scott Mowrer, the European correspondent for the *Chicago Daily News* who was about to take over as editor of the paper.

Theirs was a long and happy union. Paul turned to poetry after retiring from the newspaper business, and Hadley continued to play the piano. They both loved to fish, and they both drank and smoked more than their doctors recommended. Hadley died in 1979, having outlived Paul by eight years and Ernest by 18.

A LIFETIME BOND

Despite being a jilted woman, Hadley refused to be embittered by the way her marriage to Ernest ended. She would not say a word against him, even when encouraged to do so. When Carlos Baker interviewed her for his groundbreaking 1969 Hemingway biography, she spoke of Ernest as a "prince." Baker had his doubts about that "princeliness." Hadn't Ernest treated her shabbily, throwing her over for another—and wealthier—woman, he asked? But Hadley didn't see it that way. "He treated me just fine," she said. "It came to an end, that's all."

She also refused to think Pauline "a rotter" for stealing her husband. In her view, Pauline fell "madly in love with Ernest" and simply couldn't help herself. And Ernest too was carried away by his emotions. "[I]f someone wanted him very much, he was tremendously touched by it." Ernest might blame himself for choosing a new wife with more money, but Hadley did not condemn him for that, either.

Hadley looked back on their five-year marriage as an incredibly happy and liberating time. With Ernest's help, she had escaped her restrictive family and begun to find herself. He'd "given [her] the key to the world," she said. They'd gone off to Paris, and loved each other and had a son together. Late in her life, after Ernest had become the celebrity called Papa Hemingway (and especially after he committed suicide in 1961), reporters and biographers occasionally sought her out for comment. This brought back wonderful memories for Hadley. Yes, there were times when he was selfish and demanding and when they'd quarreled bitterly. Yet she had no regrets whatsoever, not for their magical years as husband and wife, not even for the divorce. As she told her niece, "Ernest and I never fell out of love with each other, but we couldn't live together."

The aftermath was more complicated for Ernest. He invariably thought of Hadley as the best and most admirable woman who'd ever come into his life, and he deeply regretted his disloyalty in abandoning her. This remorse struck most acutely during emotional crises in his life. At the time of his

40th birthday, in July 1939, when he was breaking up with Pauline in order to marry Martha Gellhorn, Ernest twice wrote Hadley letters of fond reminiscence. The more women he saw, he told her, the more he admired her:

Maybe we will have a fine time in Heaven, and maybe we have already had the hereafter and it was up in the Dolomites (Cortina d'Ampezzo), and the Black Forest and the forest of the Irati (near Pamplona). Well, if that is so it's O.K. with me ... Imagine if we had been born at a time when we could never have had Paris when we were young ... Good bye Miss Katherine Kat. I love you very much. It is all right to do so because it hasn't anything to do with you and that great Paul.

Weeks later, he made a point of seeing Hadley near Cody, Wyoming, where she and Paul were vacationing. Ernest arrived without advance notice, and the three of them talked for a while, mostly about Bumby. Then in December, feeling lonely as Christmastime approached, with Martha away reporting on the war in Finland and Pauline unwilling to invite him to Key West, he sent Hadley the sardonic observation that "[i]f one is perpetually doomed to marry people from St. Louis, it's best to marry them from the very best families."

With a child in common, Ernest and Hadley continued to communicate through the years by letter or telephone. In addition, he reached out to her when he felt unhappy or mistreated, confident that she would share his sorrow if not his indignation. In a very real sense, Hadley became for him in memory—as she had been in actuality—not only a loving wife, but also a nurturing mother figure who replaced the one he had been born to and repudiated.

The last time they spoke was a few months before his suicide. Ernest's health had suffered a series of blows during the previous decade. He'd always been accident-prone, and never really recovered from a series of traumatic brain injuries, particularly a London car crash in 1944 and the two plane crashes in Africa in 1954, which left him with a "concussion, a ruptured liver, spleen, and kidney, temporary loss of vision in the left eye, loss of hearing in the left ear, a crushed vertebra, a sprained right arm and shoulder, a sprained left leg, paralysis of the sphincter, and first-degree burns on his face, arms, and head." Alcoholism and depression also took their toll, and he became increasingly paranoid, sure that the IRS, the FBI, and the Immigration and

Naturalization authorities were on his trail, and that a close friend was plotting to kill him. Mentally and physically, he went downhill fast.

Worst of all, he could no longer write. In January 1961, he underwent a series of shock treatments at the Mayo Clinic in Rochester, Minnesota. Outside his room, he posted a nameplate that read "Ernest Hemingway: Former Writer." His fourth wife Mary brought him home to Ketchum, Idaho, and it was there, early in the morning of Sunday, July 2, 1961, that he stole downstairs, loaded his shotgun, propped it against his head, and tripped both barrels.

The very first story Hemingway wrote in high school ended in suicide, and he returned to the subject a number of times in his writing, most powerfully near the end of *For Whom the Bell Tolls* (1940). Ernest's father killed himself in 1929; so, years later, did his only brother, one of his four sisters and one of his granddaughters. Depression ran deep in the family, and deepest of all in Ernest himself.

Hadley, of course, knew of this, and when he called her in the spring of 1961, she feared the worst. At the time, Ernest was working on polishing and rearranging the sketches in *A Moveable Feast*, his memoir of the Paris years and by far the best work of his final decade. He wanted Hadley's help in jogging his recollections, for his memory, once a "rat-trap," was now failing. Names eluded him, and he got the dates mixed up. Ernest tried to sound cheerful over the phone, and Hadley helped as well as she could, but she sensed the sadness in his voice and knew that the man she was talking to was but a shadow of the one she'd loved and cared for. When she hung up, she burst into tears.

On May 14, Hadley read a newspaper account that Ernest was too ill to attend the memorial service for his friend Gary Cooper, whom he had come to know well during the filming of *For Whom the Bell Tolls* and as a hunting companion. She wrote Ernest then, hoping it wasn't true and enclosing a self-addressed envelope asking him to send "a calming word about health." That word never arrived.

A Moveable Feast is an odd book, half fond reminiscence and half ill-tempered attack. In it, Ernest romanticizes his own successful struggle to write and his idyllic life with Hadley, and remembers with kindness such figures as Ezra Pound and Sylvia Beach. But these sketches also include acidic portraits of such fallen-away literary friends and benefactors as Gertrude Stein, F. Scott Fitzgerald, and Ford Madox Ford, as well as damning condemnations of those he blames for destroying his and Hadley's marriage.

The book virtually idealizes poverty. When

Ernest was "belly-empty, hollow-hungry," the Cézanne paintings in the Luxembourg Museum became "sharpened and clearer and more beautiful." The tenderest moments of all evoke the joy of doing a good day's work in an unheated garret and coming home "to my wife and my son and his cat, F. Puss, all of them happy and a fire in the fireplace." That seemed perfect, but "nothing was simple there," and when the idyll didn't last he lashed out at "the rich" who'd caused the complications.

In 1927, Ernest excoriated himself for the demise of his marriage to Hadley. Thirty years later, he reassigned the blame to

> *the good, the attractive, the charming, the soon-beloved, the generous, the understanding rich who have no bad qualities and who give each day the quality of a festival and who, when they have passed and taken the nourishment they needed, leave everything deader than the roots of any grass Attila's horses' hooves have ever scoured.*

These villains go unnamed in A *Moveable Feast* but are readily identifiable as the Murphys and their coterie. Also anonymously demolished in Ernest's memoir is Pauline Pfeiffer as the infiltrating rich girl who uses "the oldest trick there is," becoming the "temporary best friend of another young woman who is married, goes to live with the husband and wife and then unknowingly, innocently and unrelentingly sets out to marry the husband." How could a young, well-meaning, dedicated young writer and devoted husband be expected to withstand such assaults?

At the end of his life, Hemingway gave up on finishing *A Moveable Feast.* Neither of the two posthumously published versions edited by his widow Mary Hemingway (1964) and his grandson Seán Hemingway (2009) does full justice to his repeated expressions of remorse and acknowledgment of guilt in passages excised from his manuscript. These present a much fairer and more sympathetic view of both Gerald and Sara Murphy, as well as of Pauline. "The rich," he wrote,

> *collected people then as some collect pictures and others breed horses and they only backed me in every ruthless and evil decision that I made ... It wasn't that the decisions were wrong although they all turned out badly from the same fault of character that made them. If you deceive and lie with one person against another you will eventually do it again. I had hated these rich because they had*

backed me and encouraged me when I was doing
wrong. But how could they know it was wrong and
had to turn out badly when they had never known all
the circumstances? It was not their fault. It was only
their fault for coming into other people's lives. They
were bad luck for people but they were worse luck to
themselves and they lived to have all of their bad luck
finally: to the very worst end that all bad luck could
go.

It was bad luck for Hemingway's reputation that this passage was not included in the 1964 *A Moveable Feast*, for, in it, he transforms himself from an unpersuasive melodramatic victim to a complex human being capable of understanding both himself and others.

The Murphys were not to blame for supporting his decision to end his first marriage, for they didn't know all the circumstances. And they themselves had the worst luck of all when two of their three children, sons Baoth and Patrick, both died in adolescence. Ernest went out of his way to visit and write Patrick during the long siege of tuberculosis that took his life, and he wrote Sara a moving letter of recollection after the boy's death.

The decision to leave Hadley derived from

deception and lying, a "fault of character" that was his as well as Pauline's and one he inevitably repeated to ensure that his second marriage also "turned out badly."

At the time of the breakup, Ernest was nearly overcome by remorse that "was never away day or night until my wife [Hadley] married a much finer man than I ever was or could be and I knew that she was happy." That lifted the cloud of guilt hovering over Pauline and himself. Then, he wrote in a passage omitted entirely from both published versions of *A Moveable Feast*, "I was happy and without any remorse and I never worked better nor was I happier and I loved the girl truly and she loved me truly and well and we had as good a life together for many years as Paris had been."

In several posthumously published works, as well as in his memoir of the Paris years, Ernest looked back on his marriage to Hadley with nostalgia and regret. The artist Thomas Hudson, protagonist of *Islands in the Stream* (1970), lives alone after two divorces. He is consumed with sorrow about having lost "Tom's mother," his first wife and the only woman he ever really loved. He remembers the blissful days in Paris when they rode their bikes through the Bois de Boulogne and drank the doubles served by the friendly waiter at the Closerie des Lilas. "But why did I ever leave Tom's mother in the first place? 'You'd better not think about that,' he told himself. That is one thing you had better not think about."

In Hemingway's "African Journal," he is on safari in Africa with his fourth wife Mary, but a dream takes him back to Hadley, filling him with remorse and guilt for how it ended.

The wife I had loved first and best and who was the mother of my oldest son was with me and we were sleeping close together to keep warm and because that was the best way to sleep if both people love each other and it is a cold night ... in the dream, I slept happily with my true love in my arms and her head firmly under my chin and when I woke I wondered about how many true loves to which you were faithful, until you were unfaithful, a man could have and I thought about the strange strictures of morality in different countries and who it was that could make a sin a sin.

When Ernest and Hadley fell in love, in 1920-21, they both were seeking escape from confining and distressing family backgrounds. Hadley gave herself with no holding back. During their five years together, she was, as needed, a lover, wife, drinking and sporting companion, and mother—to both Bumby and Ernest himself. Ernest, however, was unable to make such a total commitment. Having been deeply hurt by Agnes von Kurowsky's jilting and his mother's reprimands, he never wanted to let anyone that close again. All his life he consistently and often cruelly broke off relationships before wife or friend could do the same to him. So the marriage did not and could not last. If it hadn't been Pauline Pfeiffer, it would have been someone or something else.

Hadley nurtured Ernest and helped him grow into the great writer he became. Long after they broke up, they both remembered their marriage as the best time of their lives. The difference was that Hadley felt no regret and harbored no bitterness about their parting. It ended, that was all. They never fell out of love, but couldn't live together. Ernest found it much harder to recall the divorce without recriminations: against Pauline, the Murphys, himself. If only he'd better comprehended his own nature, he might have been less troubled. "Everything understood," as he wrote his youthful sweetheart Marjorie Bump after betraying her, "is everything forgiven."

ABOUT THE AUTHOR

Biographer and critic **Scott Donaldson** has written and edited eighteen books on 20th-century American authors, including five about Ernest Hemingway's life and work. His latest book—*The Impossible Craft: Literary Biography* (2015)—recounts the frequent trials and rare triumphs of those who write life stories of great authors.

AFTERWORD

Thank you for reading *The Paris Husband*!

If you enjoyed reading it, we would be grateful if you could help others discover and enjoy it too.

Please review it with your favorite book provider such as Amazon, BN, Kobo, iBooks, and Goodreads, among others.

Again, thank you for your support and we look forward to offering you more great reads in the future.

A Note on the Type

This book was set using Pressbooks.com on a theme named for author Annie Dillard.